WORDS OF LIGHT

PADRE PIO (1887-1968) was born Francesco Forgione, lived most of his life as a Franciscan Capuchin friar in Italy, and was canonized by Pope John Paul II in 2002. He became famous for his piety, for his counsel to pilgrims, and for the stigmata visible in his hands. He is widely recognized as the most venerated Catholic saint of the last century.

FR. RANIERO CANTALAMESSA, the editor of this volume, is a Franciscan Capuchin priest and a retired Professor of the History of Ancient Christianity at the Catholic University of Milan. Pope John Paul II appointed him Preacher to the Papal Household, a position that he still holds. His website is www.cantalamessa.org.

WORDS OF LIGHT

inspiration from the letters of

PADRE PIO

Compiled and with an Introduction by Fr. Raniero Cantalamessa

PARACLETE PRESS
BREWSTER, MASSACHUSETTS

Words of Light: Inspiration from the Letters of Padre Pio

2009 First Printing Paperback Edition
2008 First Printing Hardcover Edition

ISBN 978-1-55725-643-0

Original Title: Parole di Luce
Copyright © 1997 Edizioni "Padre Pio da PIETRELCINA", San Giovanni
Rotondo, Italy
Copyright © 1999 Ancora S.r.l.
Words of Light English edition Copyright © 2000 St. Pauls UK
Translated by Andrew Tulloch

This edition published by Paraclete Press.

The Scripture quotations found in Padre Pio's correspondence are taken from the Latin Vulgate version. At times, the Vulgate was rendered in Italian by Padre Pio and is here translated into English. For convenience, the references given are to the *Revised Standard Version of the Bible*. The Scripture quotations in other parts of this publication are from the *Revised Standard Version of the Bible*, Catholic edition, © 1965 and 1966 by the Division of Christian Education of the National Council of the Churches of Christ in the USA, and are used by permission.

The Library of Congress has catalogued the hard cover edition as follows:

Library of Congress Cataloging-in-Publication Data

Pio, of Pietrelcina, Saint, 1887–1968.
  [Correspondence. English. Selections]
  Words of light : inspiration from the letters of Padre Pio / introduced by
Father Raniero Cantalamessa.
    p. cm.
  ISBN 978-1-55725-569-3
  1. Spiritual life—Catholic Church. 2. Pio, of Pietrelcina, Saint,
1887–1968—Correspondence. 3. Capuchins—Italy—Correspondence. 4.
Catholic Church—Italy—Clergy—Correspondence. I. Title.

BX2350.3.P56313 2008
282'.092—dc22[B]   2007045061

10 9 8 7 6 5 4 3 2 1

Published by Paraclete Press
Brewster, Massachusetts
www.paracletepress.com

Printed in the United States of America

CONTENTS

Introduction		9
Introduction to the Italian Edition		15
A Short Biographical Outline		17
I	'I pray continually'	25
II	'Satan is a powerful enemy'	37
III	'I do not wish to ever offend God again'	53
IV	'I suffer and I wish always to suffer more'	65
V	'I live in a perpetual night'	81
VI	'Oh! what a beautiful thing it is to become a victim of love'	101
VII	'. . . and your neighbour as yourself'	121
VIII	'Our beautiful Virgin Mary'	134
IX	Church, Priesthood and Eucharist	141
X	Guide of Souls	154
XI	The School of Virtue	166
XII	Scattered Flowers	186
XIII	'One thing alone remains, my friend: death'	199
Coroncina to the Sacred Heart of Jesus		206

SAINT PIO OF PIETRELCINA

Born May 25, 1887
in Pietrelcina, Italy

Died September 23, 1968
in San Giovanni Rotondo, Italy

Beatified May 2, 1999 by Pope John Paul II

Canonized June 16, 2002 by Pope John Paul II

Feast Day: September 23

INTRODUCTION

My first true encounter with Padre Pio goes back to the time when I was staying at San Giovanni Rotondo in order to preach to the clergy, a number of years after his death. I hadn't known him while he was alive, nor did I feel the need, as a theologian, to deepen my knowledge of him after his death.

During that stay, I happened to read Padre Pio's own account to his confessor of how he received the stigmata, written a few days after the event; this account is on display in the apse of the older part of San Giovanni Rotondo, in the very spot where the event occurred. He ends the account making his own the words of the Psalm, 'O Lord, rebuke me not in thy anger, nor chasten me in thy wrath!'[1] The stigmata were not in his eyes, therefore, trophies of glory, but the just punishment of God for his sins. They gave him no satisfaction, but struck fear into him. They were for him what they had been for Jesus on the Cross. If we want to understand the state of soul with which Padre Pio lived his whole life with the stigmata present on his body, we need to read the whole psalm from which this verse is taken: 'For thy arrows have sunk into me... I am utterly spent and crushed; I groan because of the tumult of my heart.'[2]

---

1. Ps 38:1.
2. Ps 38:2,8.

This discovery made me want to read his letters, and in them I quickly discovered the same states of soul that were described by the great mystics. Padre Pio's own 'dark night' was in no way inferior to that described by John of the Cross; and equally the 'living flame' of his love for God dazzles the reader and allows them to catch a glimpse of another world.

St Gregory the Great said that the mark of 'greater' people is that 'in the pain of their own suffering, they do not lose sight of what might help other people; while they patiently bear the adversity that afflicts them, they still think to teach others what might be necessary; in this they are like certain great doctors who, they themselves struck, forget their own wounds in order to attend to others' (*Moralia in Job*, I, 3, 40). This description applies perfectly to Padre Pio. Inwardly assaulted throughout his life by the spirit of evil, outwardly opposed and slandered by the very people from whom he could have expected support, Padre Pio – and this is a mark of heroic sanctity – never ceased to tend to the sufferings of others, physical and spiritual, with the tenderness of a mother. Until the very last day of his life.

In the numerous debates conducted through the media on the figure of Padre Pio, secular observers sometimes make superficial judgements about him. Observing the miracles and the forms of popular devotion that surround the figure of Padre Pio, they draw the conclusion that his sanctity is that of the old style, compared with, for instance, the modern sanctity of Mother Teresa. But the saints, as saints, are neither ancient nor modern, but simply different from each other, unique. Anyone who is familiar with the biblical doctrine of the charisms will not have any difficulty in understanding why this is so: some are given the gift of learning, some charity, some the education of youth, some contemplation, and some action.

Those who claim to admire only those saints who are engaged in matters of social justice or in works of charity (not forgetting that Padre Pio himself accomplished great things in this field with his 'House for the Relief of Suffering'), effectively want to secularise sanctity. This way of thinking makes an important mistake: works of mercy are not exclusively bodily, but can be of a Spiritual kind as well. There is a charity that is no less demanding than that which tends to the sores of the body; this charity tends to the sores of a moral and Spiritual nature. This is the supreme charity which Christ exercised towards us in Gethsemane, when he took upon himself, in the form of anguish and sadness, all the sins of the world.

It is necessary to actually read the letters of Padre Pio in order to realise the stature of the man and the purity of his sanctity. Only God knows how those days were, and even more the nights, when Padre Pio left the confessional with his soul full of the sufferings and sins which had been poured into his heart. The sculptor Francis Messina, who designed the Via Crucis of San Giovanni Rotondo, portrayed Simon of Cyrene in the garments of Padre Pio. He could not have had a more beautiful intuition. Those who came to Padre Pio left the meeting feeling lighter, while he remained crushed. These are simple things that even a non-believer should, at least in part, be able to understand because they contain the human dimension of suffering and sympathy, which is well within the range of anyone's experience and precedes any talk of the supernatural.

What can be said, then, about the devotion that has blossomed around the person of Padre Pio, not only in Italy but the entire world? Some forms of this devotion, it is true, do not progress beyond a very earthly and utilitarian stage, sometimes straying into superstition. Most have a mixed approach, a little for the body and a little for the soul. But the person who follows Padre Pio's own way of internal suffering and expiation, sees in him a companion, a friend and an incomparable light.

People with all kinds of needs and desires, then, 'gather' around Padre Pio today, just as in the Gospels people of all sorts gathered round Jesus. And Jesus, who proved himself so hard against the Pharisees and the Doctors of the Law, was never scandalised by the poor who, impelled by need, turned to him. Jesus used such occasions as an opportunity to speak to them of the Kingdom of Heaven, helping them to devote themselves to a more pure and disinterested level of faith.

An enormous literature on Padre Pio already exists. Books about Padre Pio are among the very few of a religious nature that are frequently found in secular bookshops, news-stands and station kiosks. What would be the aim, then, of making available on the wider religious book market a publication that until now has only been diffused locally? I believe that this anthology fills a serious gap. Those who suspect the existence of a Padre Pio different to the one officially 'divulged' are ever more numerous, and they wish to know this Padre Pio. This little book responds to such a need in the best possible way. In the book Padre Pio finally speaks for himself, and we know how important this is for saints. We have here, in fact, thoughts, excerpts, counsels and recollections all taken from his writings. In particular, the books draws on his letters, his letters being the most faithful mirror of his soul.

Though they are indeed just such faithful mirror, it could prove quite difficult for those who lie beyond the narrow circle of the lovers of mysticism and spirituality to read them in an integrated way, a way that manages to take in all the aspects of Padre Pio's life of prayer, love and suffering they contain.

With the beatification of Padre Pio, the Friar of Pietrelcina, coming up,* it would be hard to think of a more useful contribution to making the true Padre Pio known, a thing that was very close to his own heart. Above all, this book gives us access to the fruits of the sanctity of Padre Pio. In reading it, we can partake of some of these fruits.

Fr Raniero Cantalamessa, ofm cap

---

* Translator's Note: Fr Cantalamessa wrote this introduction before the beatification, which took place on 2 May 1999.

INTRODUCTION
TO THE ITALIAN EDITION

Searching through the correspondence of Padre Pio with his Spiritual directors[3], we have chosen and arranged the pages of more intense spirituality – both theoretical and practical – that flowed from his pen. Now we present these letters in an anthology.

It was not our intention to produce a complete and thorough study of the spirituality of Padre Pio, such as could have been obtained from the first volume of his correspondence. Because this kind of systematic study is not our aim, we do not intend to develop our material in a step-by-step manner; furthermore some of the chapters contain a selection of texts that were chosen according to our personal criteria. Each chapter is a collection of texts structured around a central idea.

This anthology is intended to be a collection of the most important parts of Padre Pio's correspondence, of moments that reveal his soul, his asceticism and his mystical life.

The selected passages have been arranged in thirteen chapters, whose general contents are outlined in the introductory comment found at the head of each chapter. These observations and reflections are brief and simple, outlining the chapter and its central idea.

This book does not provide the reader with Padre

---

3. Cf. Padre Pio da Pietrelcina, *Epistolario I. Corrispondenza con i direttori spirituali (1910-1922)*, ed. Melchorre da Pobladura and Alessandro da Ripabottoni, Edizioni "Padre Pio", San Giovanni Rotondo 1971. A volume of 1,377 pages. Third edition, 1987.

Pio's full correspondence. It is, as mentioned earlier, an anthology and therefore gathers together scattered flowers, each one with its own perfume, its own beauty and colours. The reader can pick one at random, according to their taste and need, then close the book and... meditate.

From the Introduction to the first edition,
written by Fr Melchiorre da Pobladura

A SHORT
BIOGRAPHICAL OUTLINE

Parents

Padre Pio was born at Pietrelcina in the Province of
Benevento on 25 May 1887, second surviving son of
Orazio Forgione, farmer, and Guiseppa De Nuzio,
housewife. He was baptised on the following day in
the Church of St Mary of the Angels in Pietrelcina
with the name of Francesco.

The religious vocation, which Padre Pio had felt from
his earliest years, matured and at sixteen years, on 6
January 1903, he arrived at the Capuchin Priory at
Morcone. On the twenty-second of the same month
he was clothed in the Franciscan habit, taking the
name of Fra Pio, 'Brother Pius'.

On 18 July 1909 in the little Priory church at
Morcone Fra Pio was ordained deacon. For reasons of
health, Fra Pio had to suspend his studies and return
to his family in Pietrelcina. His sojourn outside the
walls of the Priory was not looked on favourably; the
Provincial, Fr Benedetto from St Mark's in Lamis,
who was also Padre Pio's Spiritual director, recalled
him a number of times, sending him to Morcone and
then to Campobasso. Obediently Fra Pio went where
he was told to, but after a short time he was constrained
to return to Pietrelcina.

Priesthood

At Benevento on 10 August 1910 Padre Pio, as he then became, was ordained priest, and on the fourteenth of the same month sang his first Mass at Pietrelcina.

During these years, Padre Pio maintained an intense correspondence with his two Spiritual fathers, Frs Benedetto and Agostino, both of St Mark's in Lamis. It is from this correspondence that we know of the Spiritual ascent undertaken by Padre Pio, an ascent consisting of both love and suffering.

On the 4 September 1916, Padre Pio was transferred to the Priory of San Giovanni Rotondo by the town of Gargano, where he was entrusted with the direction of the Seraphic Seminary.

The stigmata

In the days of the 5-7 August 1918, Padre Pio received the gift of transverberation, a Spiritual experience in which the heart is mystically pierced. A short time afterwards, on the twentieth of September, he received the gift of stigmata. He had implored the Lord to let them remain invisible, but he was not heard. He tried to hide them, but he did not succeed. At the request of the ecclesiastical authorities he was subjected to various medical examinations and check-ups.

Then began accusations and slander, against the Friars and especially against Padre Pio. The former were accused of trying to profit from the stigmata and of false publicity; the latter of deception and dubious morality.

The Way of the Cross

On 2 June 1922 the Holy Office intervened for the first time, and between 1924 and 1928 three apostolic visitors were sent to San Giovanni Rotondo.

On 23 March 1931 the Holy Office forbade Padre Pio to exercise his priestly ministry, with the exception of the Mass which, however, he had to celebrate in a chapel inside the Priory with only one attendant. On hearing the decree read out, Padre Pio raised his eyes to heaven and said, 'Let God's will be done'.

So Padre Pio began a life of complete isolation.

Padre Pio takes up the ministry once more

After two years of prohibition, on 14 July 1933, the Holy Office returned Padre Pio's licence to him, which enabled him to celebrate in public and hear confessions once again.

So Padre Pio began a new rhythm of life. He said Mass very quickly, normally taking about one and a half hours. A long thanksgiving after communion concluded, he heard confessions of both men and women. In the afternoon he heard the confessions of a few men, and the rest of the time he spent meditating and praying.

The Casa Sollievo della Sofferenza ('House for the Relief of Suffering') and the Gruppi di preghierar ('Prayer Groups')

On the 9 January 1940 in his little cell, Padre Pio and doctors Carlo Kiswarday and Mario Sanvico came up with the idea for the construction of the *Casa Sollievo della Sofferenza*. On 19 March 1947 work began, and the idea became reality.

On 26 July 1954 the outpatient departments were open, and on 5 May 1956 the solemn inauguration took place in the presence of Cardinal Giacomo Lercaro. According to the Instructions of Padre Pio, the *Casa Sollievo della Sofferenza* had to offer the same treatment to persons poor and rich alike.

Another deeply Spiritual and charitable work which Padre Pio began, was the foundation of the *Gruppi di preghiera*. In the mind of Padre Pio these groups were to be places where faith is nurtured, hotbeds of charity, where Christ himself is present every time the group meets for prayer and fraternal *agape* under the guidance of their pastors and Spiritual directors.

Whilst these two great works of Padre Pio grew and developed, one for the relief of the body and the other for the relief of the soul, Padre Pio himself strove to climb the high peak of contemplation through internal and external suffering. The whole of Padre Pio's life was characterised by the mystical state known as the 'dark night'.

Further suffering for Padre Pio

On 12 May 1947, during a canonical visit the Father General of the Order noticed certain 'abuses' committed by the so-called 'holy women' in Church and near the confessional of Padre Pio. He left some instructions aimed at remedying these abuses.

Around 1960 the complaints, accusations and appeals began again, particularly because of the fanaticism of some jealous 'followers' of the Friar. It went as far as the placement of microphones and tape recorders in Padre Pio's cell and certain parlours. So on 30 July 1960 another Apostolic Visitor arrived at San Giovanni Rotondo. Following this canonical visit, some heavy restrictions were placed on Padre Pio's exercise of his apostolic ministry; he accepted them in a spirit of humility and obedience.

On 30 January 1964, Cardinal Ottaviani communicated to the supervisors of Padre Pio's Order the will of the Holy Father Paul VI: Padre Pio was to be allowed full liberty in the exercise of his ministry.

The death of Padre Pio

On 7 July 1968 Padre Pio had a severe collapse. From then on his health became continually worse.

On Sunday 22 September 1968, the fiftieth anniversary of Padre Pio's stigmata was solemnly celebrated with an international meeting of the *Gruppi di preghiera*. Padre Pio, by now worn out, celebrated the solemn sung Mass.

Towards midnight on 22 September, Padre Pio's condition worsened even further. He called his Superior. He confessed himself and received the sacrament of the sick. He asked forgiveness from his confreres for all the annoyances and scandals he had caused. He asked to be dressed in the religious habit and to be made comfortable in an armchair. Towards 2.30 in the morning of 23 September 1968, he breathed his last, ending his life in a holy manner. After his death it was noticed that the stigmata had disappeared without leaving the slightest scar.

The solemn funeral took place on the evening of Thursday 26 September. He was then interred in the crypt of the Church of Santa Maria delle Grazie at San Giovanni Rotondo.

The tomb of Padre Pio is now the destination of a continuous stream of pilgrims and faithful who come from all parts of the world to pray and ask for grace.

On 20 March 1983 the process for Padre Pio's beatification was initiated. The ecclesiastical Tribunal was set up at San Giovanni Rotondo in the sanctuary of Santa Maria delle Grazie, and it brought its labours to a close on Sunday 21 January 1990. In seven years it questioned 73 witnesses and collected an imposing documentation of some 104 volumes, which was handed over to the Congregation for the Causes of the Saints. On 13 June 1997 the consultants delivered a favourable opinion regarding the heroism of the virtues practised by Padre Pio. John Paul II proclaimed Padre Pio 'Blessed' on 2 May 1999 and canonized him on 16 June 2002.

WORDS OF LIGHT

I

'I PRAY CONTINUALLY'

(*Letters,* volume I, p. 751)*

The attitude that best characterises Padre Pio is perhaps that of a 'pray-er'. His earthly day was spent in uninterrupted conversation with God. The irresistible appeal of his person and the overwhelming aura radiated by his priestly activity, could not be understood if detached from his vision of intimate, vital and personal contact with the Father who is in heaven. In fact, it is through the prism of prayer and contemplation that all regarding the stigmatic of Gargano becomes clear; all is illumined and explained; his mission need no longer be a puzzle to the men and women who live in an age of material well-being, technology and secularisation.

The vigorous brushstroke used by Tommaso da Celano in his Spiritual portrait of St Francis is a masterly one: 'Totus non tam orans quam oratio' (prayer rather than praying). Much the same could be said of Padre Pio, and the affirmation that he was a 'man of prayer' is not an emotional exaggeration or a topic for literary discussion, but rather an unequivocal judgement demonstrated by the facts, documents and

---

* Here, and after each of the excerpts in the following pages, the reference is to the Italian first volume of Padre Pio's collected letters. This book, mentioned in the Introduction to the first edition above, contains Padre Pio's correspondence with his Spiritual directors and runs to 1,377 pages.

the experience of all those who knew him. The life of prayer was the centre of gravity for his apostolate and the keystone of his Spiritual dwelling.

In this chapter we have gathered together those passages which more directly and importantly touch on the subject of prayer. The passages were not written – it is worth repeating – with the aim of producing a complete and comprehensive treatment of prayer, in all its different forms and with all its different levels. The passages tell not of theoretical principles, but of lived experiences. Nevertheless, these pages that follow contain sure guidance and well-grounded suggestions for everyone's life, whether they be masters or disciples in the Spiritual life.

1 My ordinary way of praying is this. No sooner have I set myself to pray than I immediately feel my soul begin to recollect itself in a peace and tranquillity that cannot be expressed in words. The senses remain suspended, with the exception of the hearing, which sometimes is not suspended. Normally this sense does not cause any bother, however, and I must confess that even if I were to be surrounded by a deafening noise, I would not be in the least disturbed. From this you will be able to understand that there are few times that I manage to discourse with the intellect during my prayer (420).

2 Time seems to fly past and it never seems that I have enough of it for prayer. I feel a great love of good reading, but I read little enough because both my ill-health prevents me, and also because on opening

a book and reading for a little, I become so profoundly recollected that reading becomes prayer (422).

3 I never tire of praying to Jesus. It is true that my prayers are worthy rather of punishment than reward, because I have sickened Jesus too much by my numberless sins; but in the end he will be moved to have mercy on me (209).

4 I want to tell you about a curious thing that has been happening to me for some time now, though I don't really give it much thought.

In prayer it happens that I forget to pray for those who commend themselves to me (not all, however), or for those who I intended to pray for. I strive beforehand to make myself pray and commend such a person or another; but of course, O Lord! as soon as I enter into prayer, my mind rests in a perfect emptiness, and not a trace remains of what was there before, even though I had it very much at heart.

At other times, on the other hand, I feel moved, standing in prayer, to pray for those I had no intention of praying for and, what is even more marvellous, for those who I have never known, nor seen, nor heard of, nor have they commended themselves to me, not even through other people. And sooner or later the Lord always answers these prayers (443).

5 As soon as I set myself to pray, I immediately feel as if my heart has been engulfed by the flame of a living love. This flame has nothing to do with any flame in this world here below. It is a delicate and sweet flame that gives no pain. It is so sweet and so delicious that the spirit finds a great satisfaction in it, and remains satisfied by it in such a way that it does

not lose the desire for it. It is, O God! the most marvellous thing for me, and perhaps I will never understand it until I enter the heavenly homeland.

This desire, far from taking away the soul's complete satisfaction, continually refines it. The enjoyment that the soul feels in its centre rather than being diminished by the desire, becomes more and more perfected. The same can be said of the desire to delight always in this most living flame, because such a desire is not quenched by the delight, but is refined by it. From this you will be able to understand the times when I can discourse with the intellect or make use of the functionings of the senses are being ever more rare.

I don't know whether I've managed to explain myself, but I don't know how to express myself more clearly. The soul which has been placed in such a state by the Lord, enriched by so much heavenly knowledge, ought to be more eloquent; and yet this is not so in my case, my soul has become almost mute. I do not know if this phenomenon is true only in me. In terms that are very general, and more often than not also empty of meaning, the soul manages to express a little bit of what the Spouse of the soul is doing in it. Believe me, my Father, all this is no light torment for the soul.

What happens in this situation is similar to what would happen to a poor shepherd boy if he was brought into a royal chamber, where an array of precious objects had been gathered together, the like of which he had never seen before. When the shepherd boy leaves the chamber he would undoubtedly have all those various precious and beautiful objects present in his mind's eye, but he would also undoubtedly not be able to say how many there were, nor to give them their proper names. He would want to speak to others about all he had seen; he would gather together all his powers of reasoning in order to explain himself well. But seeing that all his efforts were unavailing, he would end up preferring to keep quiet.

This is what is happening in my soul which, through divine goodness alone, has been raised to this level of prayer.

Alas, my father, I realise well, of course, that we do not always deserve what we get!

All these extraordinary things, far from ceasing, become continually more and more lofty. I feel that the raptures have become stronger, and they usually come with such force that all my efforts to prevent them come to nothing. The Lord has placed my soul in a greater detachment from the things of this world here below, and I feel that he is continually strengthening it in the holy freedom of spirit (461).

6 The purely supernatural revelations and apparitions concern God, his perfections and attributes. I find it impossible to describe them in writing, even though I have them present in my mind just as I have in my hands this piece of paper on which I am now writing.

An example I hope might make this clearer in a limited way. We carry a mirror around in front of us. What do we see? Nothing other than a human image. Our intellect, if it is not infirm, does not doubt, and would not even dream of doubting, that the image is our own.

Let us imagine that all the world wants to prove to us that we are fooling ourselves in our belief that the image we see is our own; would they perhaps manage, not to remove our conviction, but to cause even a slight doubt to raise itself in our minds about it? Certainly not.

Well, the same things happens to me regarding these divine revelations and locutions. The soul sees these heavenly secrets, these divine perfections, these divine attributes, very much more clearly than we see our image in the mirror. All the efforts I make to doubt their reality, succeed only in making my soul ever stronger in its conviction. I don't know whether you've ever seen what happens when a little water is poured over a great fire. This small amount of water not only does not put the fire out, but actually feeds the flame.

This is what happens to me after all my attempts to doubt that these things come from God.

But let us return to the image that we observed in the mirror. We cannot separate that image from the mirror, much less can we touch it. And yet the image exists outside of us, but not without us.

The same happens to me. The soul remains itself, fundamentally convinced that the heavenly revelations could only come from God, notwithstanding all its continuing efforts to doubt this fact. But as we find it impossible to separate the image from the mirror or to touch it, it is equally even more difficult for me to be able to write about these heavenly secrets, because of the lack of words to describe them. The soul without being mistaken can only state what these things are not.

I'll try to make myself clear. Let us suppose that God reveals to the soul one of his attributes, his holiness for example. The soul understands this attribute, in as far as God has given it the capacity; that which it has once understood it has always fixed inside it, but it is not able to express that which it has understood and that which it also sees.

But if others speak of this divine attribute, the soul

understands very well and very quickly if they make a mistake or speak in an imperfect way.

This way of speaking may seem incomprehensible to you, but if the Lord has given you some experience in this matter, you will know that I am speaking the truth. If you find this sort of language obscure, my Father, I declare that I don't know how to explain myself more clearly, unless Jesus wished to come to my aid. O father, who could sketch out a faithful image of these things? I would greatly desire to do this, if only to know from you what this state is in which my soul more and more finds itself at present. Patience! Blessed be the God who alone can do great things! (373).

7 Oh, if praying for other people did not include also praying for oneself, my soul would undoubtedly be the most neglected of all; and this is not because it does not recognise its need of divine help, but because it lacks the time to present all its necessities to the Lord! This seems ridiculous, and yet this is how it normally is with me (531).

8 May it please the Lord, source of all life, not to deny me this water – so sweet and so precious – that he in the exuberance of his love for humankind promises to those who thirst for it. I thirst for it, O my Father, for this water; I ask Jesus for it with continual groans and sighs. Pray yourself also, that he doesn't hide it from me; tell him, Father, so that he knows how great my need for that water is, that alone can heal a soul wounded by love.

Let this most tender Spouse of the sacred Canticle console a soul that thirsts for him, and let him console it with that same divine kiss which the holy spouse requested of him. Tell him that until a soul receives this kiss, it will never be able to conclude a pact with him in these terms: 'I am my beloved's and my beloved is mine'[4] (699).

9 The storm wants to submerge me, and I fear that sometimes I have already been submerged. Nothing is able to lighten the thick darkness in which I am immersed. It seems that the waters of tribulation might suffocate me at any moment.

I feel that both my physical and moral forces are exhausted. I pray, but no ray of light comes from on high. My continual asking for help from the Most High parches my throat. My God, who will free me from this dreadful prison, from this double inferno? My Father, since my praying is of no avail, ah! for the sake of charity do me the favour of asking God again and again to show me his mercy (1256).

10 Heaven, I think, is closed to me, and every impulse of spirit and every sigh I send there returns in the company of some thunderbolt to wound my poor heart. My prayer seems to be vain, and my battered spirit finds when it draws near yet again to try and gain access once more, that it is powerless to reach the very one who clothes it with courage and power. It finds itself reduced to this nothingness because it is unable to take any more risks, even though a little later it will once more take a risk and find itself reduced to the same powerlessness (1073).

---

4.   Song 6:3.

11 My prayer, my Father, is the sting of mortal griefs and pains, horrible to think about again. I don't understand anything anymore, I don't know if my prayers are prayers, or powerful feelings of resentment that the heart addresses to its God in the fullness of its grief. I feel a forsaken emptiness inside me, horrible to think about when one is immersed in it. All there is, is nothingness, the perfect nothingness, except for the very rare lamps of uncertain light flashing in the thick darkness in which I am immersed, that say to the spirit, 'God is in the good!' But God remains hidden from the attentive spirit that burns itself up keeping watch for him, that is compelled to seek for him, though the task is exhausting. Finding itself alone in a desolate solitude the poor spirit goes on consuming itself through the many fears of offending him since it is alone with its ardent character; alone with inner and outer vexations; alone with its natural corruption; alone with the trials of the enemy. My Good, where are you? I do not know you anymore nor can I find you; but this searching for you is a necessity, you who are the life of the soul that dies. My God, my God!… I do not know how to say anything else: 'Why have you abandoned me?' (Mk. 15:34). With the exception of this abandonment I know absolutely nothing about anything, not even about life, which I do not know how to live (1029).

12 But how can I repay all that has been done for me? The answer, unfortunately, is a very painful one for me: to repay all with prayer to the Lord. That's fine, and that's what I do. But you must also agree with me that in this I am bound by many other chains. And then, what value can the prayer of one who prays in a sepulchre of death, of one whom the Lord remembers

no more, ever have? I pray continually, but my prayer does not rise above this world here below. Heaven, my Father, seems to have become made of bronze; an iron hand is placed on my head; this hand pushes me continually further and further away. In some moments it seems to me that my soul is on the point of seizing the object of its yearning. But who would believe it? The object which has been torturing my soul thus, suddenly hides itself from it, and with a hand, a cruel hand I would say, pushes me far away (751).

13 I find, O Father, your proposal completely to my liking – that is, that we unite ourselves in our intention and help each other in prayer. In all bad weather you will find me before him from half-past four until about half-past nine; there I am at all times from quarter to eleven until towards the Hail Mary. The remainder depends on circumstances (678).

14 It happens to me, for a long time now, that when Jesus comes, those things that I had very much at heart to ask him fly away and I remember only what Jesus wants me to remember. It also normally happens to me that when he comes, I feel compelled by an irresistible impulse to pray and commend to him persons whom I have never seen and who I have never heard talked of, to ask for these those graces that have never passed through my mind. To tell the truth, it has never happened when I pray in this way that the Lord leaves one of my petitions unanswered.

I'm not as surprised by this second mystery as I am amazed at the first. Sometimes I start to cry like a baby because I don't remember to ask Jesus for that which I have so much at heart. How this happens, I cannot understand. I greatly fear the deceit of the enemy. And who knows, I go away thinking, if I am not already in the net of the enemy.

To all I have said up to now we must add the fact that this business has, for a short time, been becoming more usual than ever. Father, believe me, one of the many thorns that contribute to making the martyrdom still more harsh is exactly this. You cannot imagine how much affliction and desolation this new thorn gives me (590).

15 How is it, O Father, that when I am with Jesus, all that I have the intention and resolute will to ask him never comes to mind? Nevertheless I feel a very acute pain on account of this forgetfulness of mine. How can it be explained? Until now no one has been able to fully convince me.

Listen, then, to a very strange thing. When I am with Jesus, it happens that I request of Jesus things that I never had in mind to present to him, and also for persons that not only have I never had in mind, but – and this causes me great wonder – persons such as I have never known and never heard talk of. And here it must be observed that, when this happens to me, I have never known Jesus not to give to these persons those things which I requested for them (570).

16 Let them fear nothing; the Lord is with them. Assure them that I never forget, in my nothingness, to commend them continually to the Lord and that I pray more for them than for me; and the Lord knows if I am lying.

The reason why I pray less for myself, lies not in virtue, dear Father, but rather in my unworthiness that makes me resist asking for more graces, being that I become increasingly more undeserving as these heavenly favours grow.

Pray for me and get these two angelic butterflies* to pray for me. If I do reach salvation, I will owe everything (after the divine mercy!) to the prayers of these holy souls (435).

---

* Translator's Note: Padre Pio is presumably writing about two people he knew.

II

'SATAN IS A POWERFUL ENEMY'

(*Letters,* volume I, p. 924)

The record of Satan's relentless attacks, without respite or the sparing of blows, presents us with some of the more disturbing pages from Padre Pio's biography. In terms of intensity and variety, it is not easy to find its counterpart in Catholic writings on the saints. The case of Padre Pio is a rare one, albeit not unique.

The enemy, in his underhand strategy, applies himself to tormenting the body and tempting the spirit. Not seldom, he appears in frightening forms and is pitiless on the senses, causing dreadful things to happen to the body. At other times, his assaults are directed at the powers of the soul, in order to prevent the exercise of the Theological virtues and the progress in love of God.

The bodily torments strike terror and fear into those who suffer them, and the Spiritual temptations generate confusion and push the soul towards the precipice of desperation. In God's plan, both of these cases have the well-defined purpose of purification and elevation.

Padre Pio, illumined by grace and sustained by the authority of his directors, realised all this. For this reason the severe and daily struggle could not turn him from the right path, nor could it arrest his steps towards the summit of perfection. He did not go back, but he challenged the enemy forces, confiding always in the help of the Lord, of Mary most holy, and of his guardian angel. Victory always smiled on him, even if it was gained at a high price.

The collection of passages that we here present, offer some vivid descriptions of the struggles Padre Pio maintained with Satan and his satellites; but above all they reveal the intensity of the purifying trial and the supernatural strategy required to assure victory in it.

⚜

17 When has Satan ever told the truth for the good of a soul? (1183).

18 When will it be, O my dear Father, that Jesus will consume me completely in his love? When can I be consumed completely by the divine flame? When can I unite myself fast to him so that I can break out into a completely new song, the song of victory? When will this struggle inside me, between Satan and my poor soul finish, as my soul wants to belong completely to her heavenly Spouse? The weakness of my being makes me tremble and break out into a cold sweat (923).

19 Will it ever be that I rest in the arms of Jesus, and he be mine and I totally his? This is, unfortunately, a question that springs spontaneously to my lips.

When I received your recent letter, those *Cossacks*, before I had opened it, told me to tear it up, or to throw it in the fire. If I had torn it up, they would have withdrawn for ever, and would have never molested me any more.

I remained silent, not giving them any reply, though scorning them in my heart.

Then they added, 'We want this simply as a condition for our withdrawal. If you do it, you will not be scorning anyone.'

I replied that nothing could move me from my resolve. They hurled themselves on my back like ravenous tigers, cursing me and threatening that they would make me pay.

My Father, they have kept their word! From that day onwards, they have beaten me daily. But I am not frightened; don't I have in Jesus a father? Is it not true that I am always his son? I can confidently say that Jesus has never forgotten me, even when I was far from him. He has followed me everywhere with his love (334).

20 My ill-health continues as usual with its highs and lows. I do suffer, it's true, but I am very cheerful because even in the midst of suffering the Lord does not cease to make me feel an inexpressible · joy. If it were not, my Father, for the war that the devil wages continually, I would be almost in paradise. I find myself in the hands of the devil, who strives to wrench me from the hands of Jesus. So much war, my God, this one wages on me! (208).

21 *Bluebeard* follows, with divine permission, to wage war against me; but God is with me (343).

22 Besides the trial of Spiritual fears and agitations, with just a whiff of desolation, Jesus adds that long and varied trial of physical malaise, using to this end those horrible *Cossacks*.

Listen to what I had to suffer a few evenings ago from those impure apostates. The night was already advanced; they began their assault with a dreadful noise, and although I saw nothing at the beginning, I understood who was producing this very strange noise; and rather than becoming frightened I prepared myself for the fight by placing a mocking smile on my lips for them. Then they appeared under the most abominable forms, and to entice me to lose my resolve they began to treat me courteously. But, thanks be to Heaven, I told them off good and proper, treating them for what they were. When they saw that their efforts were coming to nothing, they hurled themselves at me, they threw me on the ground and struck me again and again, launching pillows, books, chairs into the air, at the same time emitting desperate shrieks and uttering extremely dirty words. Luckily the rooms on either side of where I am, and also those below, are not being used.

I complained to my Guardian Angel about this, who, after having preached a nice little homily to me, added, 'Give thanks to Jesus, that he treats you as one chosen to follow him closely up the steep slope of Calvary. I see, soul entrusted to my care by Jesus, with joy and emotion inside me, Jesus' conduct towards you. Do you think that you would be so happy, if you weren't so worn out? I, who in holy charity greatly desire what is best for you, rejoice ever more deeply to see you in this state. Jesus permits the devil these assaults, so that your devotion might make you dear to him, and he wants you to become like him during the anguish in the desert, the garden and the cross. Defend yourself, always drive off these malign insinuations and scorn them; and where your strength is of no use, do not worry, delight of my heart, I am close to you!' (330).

23 Oh, for charity's sake, do not deny me your help, do not deny me your teaching, knowing that the devil continues more than ever to act with ferocity against the little boat of my poor spirit. My Father, I can't take any more of it; I feel all my strength dwindling. The battle really is in its last phase; every moment I feel suffocated by the waters of tribulation.

Ah me, who will save me? I fight alone, day and night, against such a strong and powerful enemy. Who will win? On whom will victory smile? Both parties fight hard. When I measure the strength of both parties, I see myself weak, I see myself worn out in front of the enemy ranks; I am on the point of being crushed, of being reduced to nothing.

In short, all things considered, it seems to me that I should be the one who is vanquished. But what am I saying! Is it possible that the Lord will permit it? Never! I feel, in the deepest part of my spirit, a giant rising to its feet again – the strength to cry forcefully to the Lord: 'Lord, save us! We are perishing!'[5] (549).

24 But may the most high God always be blessed, who has never completely abandoned me into the hands of the powers of darkness! Just when it seems that the battle is soon to be concluded in favour of my adversaries, with great speed the Lord comes, to put them to flight and reduce all of them to impotence. May the divine mercy live forever!

How good Jesus is towards his creatures! How many victories can this poor servant count, all due to his most powerful help! Jesus has desired to make me

---

5.   Mt 8:25; 14:30; Lk 8:24.

an example of his grace, and to put me forward as an example for sinners, so that they don't despair of their salvation (512).

25 The weakness of my being fills me with fear and brings me out in cold sweat. Satan with his malign arts never tires of waging war on me, and of trying to storm the little fortress by assaulting it from every direction. In short, Satan is for me a powerful enemy, who when he resolves to take a piazza by storm, does not content himself with assaulting it under the cover of a smokescreen or by directing his efforts at a single bastion; he assaults the whole of it from every side, everywhere he torments it.

My Father, the malign arts of Satan terrify me; but from God alone, through Jesus Christ, I hope for the grace always to attain the victory and never be defeated (924).

26 The devil assiduously makes a deafening noise and roars around my poor will. In this state I can do nothing other than say with firm resolution, though without resentment, 'Long live Jesus! I believe...!' But who can tell you how I actually say these holy expressions? I say them with timidity, without strength and without courage, and I must do great violence to myself. Tell me, Father, is it possible, is my present state compatible with the presence of God in my soul? Isn't it perhaps the effect of God's withdrawal from my soul? My Father, I beg you, talk to me once again with all frankness and sincerity. Suggest to me the way I should conduct myself so that I don't offend the Lord, and tell me if there is hope for me, if God will return to this soul (838).

27 In this hellish chaos the only thing I can see and hear is the roaring of ferocious lions, who are always ready to devour their prey (996).

28 My God! Those malign spirits, my Father, try everything to make me lose my way; it seems that they take advantage of my physical weakness to vent their malice even more on me, and to see if, in this state, it is possible to wrench me from the bosom of that faith and that strength that comes to me from the Father of Lights.

At certain moments I find myself right on the edge of a precipice; it seems to me that the battle might be about to turn in favour of those scoundrels; I feel that just everything, everything shakes me; a mortal agony passes through my poor spirit, pouring itself over my poor body as well, and all its members become numb. The life that lies before me seems to be brought to a halt: it is suspended (497).

29 I spent a terrible night, the night before last. Those *Cossacks* did nothing but strike me continually from towards 10 o'clock, when I went to bed, until 5 o'clock in the morning. They put many diabolical suggestions before me: thoughts of desperation, of a lack of trust in God. But long live Jesus! I protected myself by saying again and again to Jesus: 'vulnera tua, merita mea'.[6]

I really began to believe that this was actually the last night of my existence or that, even if I didn't die, that I would lose my reason. But blessed be Jesus, nothing like that happened.

---

6. 'Your wounds are my merits.'

At five in the morning, when those *Cossacks* had gone away, a coldness took possession of my whole person; it made me tremble from head to foot, like a reed exposed to a raging wind. I was in this state for a couple of hours. I bled from the mouth.

Finally the Child Jesus came, and I told him that I wanted only to do his will. He consoled me and he reassured me about the suffering I experienced during the night. O God, how my little heart beat, how my cheeks burnt near this heavenly Child! (292).

30 I cannot steady my spirit sufficiently to enable me to tell you all that has been happening to me recently, since during this time the devil has been waging war on me more intensely than ever. I am not able to repulse the deceptions that the enemy of salvation directs against me.

Who then, my Father, will free me from so many temptations and from so many anxieties? Who will console me? Who would believe that even during the hours of rest one might be anxious? Well, my Father, I can assure you that even these hours have become very bitter to me. I find a little peace in thinking and reading your teachings. But these are brief instants, as the enemy is always vigilant, always present right from the start.

The Spiritual struggles, compared with what I am suffering in the body, are very much greater, though even the bodily suffering itself increases continually. I would wish, dear Father, I do not ask for a lot, for at least one hour of rest a day. But let the most holy and most loveable will of God always be done in me, and all round me, in all and for all, because this is what has been my support.

The devil wants me for himself at any cost. If I were not Christian, all that I am suffering would lead me to believe myself to be already overcome. I do not know for what reason God has not yet been moved to pity me and free me from it; I know only this, however, that he does not work in us without most holy aims which are for our benefit.

And now, Father, for the love of Jesus Christ and of our beautiful and sorrowful Virgin, if I have something in my heart that does not please God, even though it be small, tell me about it so that I can tear it out, regardless of cost. Who knows if this suffering that God has permitted might not be a punishment for the things still in me that sicken him. If I do not first remove these will God not be moved to pity?

I am sure that you, knowing me to be in so much wretchedness, will pray to the Lord for me so that he might at least spare me the Spiritual struggles, as the causes for offending him are many. The prayer, of course, has the usual condition: if it be for the greater glory of his divine majesty and the advantage of my soul (212).

31 The Apostle James exhorts souls to rejoice when they are harassed by various storms and numerous contradictions: 'My brothers and sisters, whenever you face trials of any kind, consider it nothing but joy'.[7] The reason is that in the struggle there is the crown, and the more the soul fights the more the palms of victory multiply. Knowing that every victory gained corresponds to a level of eternal glory, how, O Father, can one not rejoice to see oneself committed to gaining many during the course of one's life? (1011).

---

7. Jas 1:2.

32 I do not know how to thank our dear Jesus, who gives me much strength and courage to bear not only the many infirmities that he sends me, but also the continuous temptations which he, unfortunately, allows and which go on multiplying from day to day. These temptations make me tremble from head to foot at the thought of offending God. I hope that the future may at least resemble the past in that I do not become a victim of them. My Father, this suffering is too much for me. I implore the Lord that he might at least deign to change it for some other, even at the cost of doubling it (200).

33 You know very well that my Spiritual wars are very many and this certainly wouldn't worry me, if I could know whether or not I was free of offending God. But what really worries me is not being able to tell whether I have consented to the temptations or not.

Truly, I am currently resolved rather to willingly give myself up to be torn into a thousand pieces, than to let myself offend God one single time. I turn to my confessor, and there I get a little peace. But a little later, here we are once again. It seems to me that at times I feel the need for confession but have hardly anything to say to the confessor, I remember nothing specific. Also at the altar, my Father, God alone knows how much violence I need to do to myself to avoid sinning again (278).

34 It is also true, however, that the devil gives himself no peace in his efforts to make me loose peace of soul, and to lessen the great trust I have in divine mercy. He principally strives to obtain this through continual temptations against holy purity

which he causes to arise in my imagination without ceasing and even, at times, through a simple glance at things which if not holy, are at least indifferent. All of this I laugh at, like something not worth bothering about, following your advice. It does distress me, however, in certain moments, that I am not certain whether at the first assault of the enemy I was ready to resist. I am certain that as I examine myself now, I would prefer death rather than deliberately offend my dear Jesus with a single sin, however light (196).

35 There are certain moments in which I am assailed by violent temptations against the faith. I am certain that the will is not moved, but the imagination is so inflamed and presents the temptation in such bright colours, that the mind wanders, and sin is presented as a thing that is not only indifferent, but delightful. From here those thoughts arise – thoughts of discouragement, of suspicion and even, do not be horrified Father, for charity's sake, blasphemous thoughts.

I am terrified when faced with such a struggle; I tremble and force myself always, and I am certain that, through the grace of God, I do not fall (910).

36 In recent days my soul has yet again descended into hell; yet again the Lord has exposed me to the fury of Satan. I mean that this infamous apostate wants to tear from my heart that which is most sacred in it: faith. By day he assails at all times; he makes sleep bitter to me by night.

Up to this moment of my writing, I have a full awareness that I have yielded nothing to him; but in the future? I feel that my will is attached firmly to its God, but I must also confess that my physical and moral strength becomes weaker and weaker because of the continual struggle (966).

37 My spirit is continually caught up in the darkness, which becomes ever thicker. The temptations against the faith continue to grow and grow. I live, therefore, always in the dark; I try to see, but in vain. My God, when will I see you arise, I don't expect the sun, but at least the dawn? I am sustained by the word of authority alone. *Fiat voluntas Dei!* (988).

38 Satan stands near me diligently with his energetic suggestions. I make every effort to combat him but I am aware that I am powerless to know how to free myself from him with a more vigorous will. Furthermore, and I fear that there is something that Satan has already won from me, because I see him always around me and he always returns to the assault. There is, therefore, something that he has already won and something that he hopes still to win.

My God, is it possible that my existence continually sickens you? The assault advances, my Father, and strikes me at the centre; it appears that even holy obedience, the ultimate voice remaining to hold the crumbling fort, might itself fall under Satan's influence.

I want to believe in this voice at any cost and I act as if I believe, not knowing whether this belief remains on my lips or is rooted in my will. But this voice of obedience drowns in the fury of all my anxieties and torments; and after the immediate comfort that comes from this voice, the soul feels itself plummet into an even more pitiless bitterness and takes large gulps from the chalice of bitterness, with no comfort and not knowing why and for whom it suffers (1074).

39 When I sit down to consider the great battles won with divine help against the devil, I count so many that they cannot be numbered. Who knows how many times, if God had not stretched out his hand to me, my faith would have wavered, my hope and my charity lessened, and how many times my intellect would have become darkened if Jesus, eternal sun, had not illumined it! I acknowledge all to be the work of his infinite love. He has denied me nothing; rather, I must clearly state that he has given me more than I have asked of him (317).

40 The deceptions of the devil continue to afflict my soul. The fact remains, however, that I have noticed for some days now a Spiritual joy that cannot be explained. I do not know its cause. I do not feel anymore the many difficulties that I once did in resigning myself to what God wishes of me. Rather I repel the deceitful calumnies of the tempter with an ease, neither wearied nor tired by my efforts. But is this a good or a bad sign? Passing through my head is the thought that the cause of this might be a cooling of the love of God in me. You can imagine how bitter this thought is to me (230).

41 The spectacle is very sad and sorrowful: only he who has been put to the test can imagine it. How hard is the test, my Father, that places us in grave risk of offending our Saviour and Redeemer! Yes, here one risks all for all. Will the compassionate Lord continue to be merciful towards me? Will he continue to give me that strength and constancy which up to the present he has given me, so that I am able always to conquer and subdue this enemy of ours who is so strong and powerful? (498).

42 Even in these holy days the enemy strives with all his might to induce me to consent to his evil plans. This malign spirit attempts to place thoughts of impurity and desperation in my heart, employing in particular every sort of illusion. He continually holds up for my inspection, a picture which is painted in the most worldly of colours and contains the most gloomy of perspectives, the picture of my life. In a word, my Father, I find myself right in the hands of the devil, who would with all his efforts like to snatch me from the hands of Jesus. Therefore I am fighting him alone and I find myself with a heart full of fear. I do not know what will happen to me. I feel very weak in soul and body, my Father, but I abandon myself to God. If this is the will of God I want to suffer more and more in order to please him (219).

43 If it were not, my Father, for the war that the devil continually wages against me I would be almost in Paradise. I am in the hands of the devil, who strives to snatch me from the arms of Jesus. How intense is the war he wages against me! In certain moments I'm not far from loosing my head because of the continual violence that I must do to myself. How many tears, how many sighs, my Father, have I addressed to heaven in order to be free of him. But it doesn't matter, I'll not tire of praying to Jesus. It is true that my prayers are worthy rather of punishment than reward, because I have sickened Jesus too much by my numberless sins. But in the end he will have pity on me by taking me from the world and calling me to himself, or by freeing me from it. And if neither of these two graces be granted to me, I hope at least that the grace of not giving into temptation may be (209).

44 Well, the Spiritual warfare does not cease, rather it becomes more severe. In short, my Father, the enemy of our salvation is so angry that he leaves me hardly a moment of peace, fighting me in various ways. I desire from Jesus the grace to be liberated from the fear that I have offended him, and I desire that if he wishes to mortify me, that he mortify me through bodily pains, which I would accept willingly (206).

45 Who will free me from the miseries in which I find myself? More temptations than ever are being launched against me. They afflict me greatly, not because of the continual violence I must do to myself, but because of the ugliness and continual hostility I experience, and because of the great fear of offending God in every moment, since there are moments in which I find myself right on the edge of a precipice, ready to fall. Even during the hours of rest the devil does not cease to afflict my soul in various ways.

It is true that in the past I have been strong by the grace of God and not given in to the deceits of the enemy; but who knows what will happen in the future? Yes, I would like a moment of truce from Jesus. But let his will be done in me! (203).

46 It is true that the temptations to which I am subject are very great, but I trust in divine providence not to fall into the noose of the deceiver (198).

47 The devil, meanwhile, makes use of this weakening of strength and my inability to react to afflict me even more with phantasms and bogey men. But, my Father, what can be the aims of God

that he allow the devil so much freedom? I am almost carried off by desperation. Yet you must believe me, my Father, I have no desire to displease God. I don't know how to account for, and much less understand, how such a resolute will, ready to do good, can be found in company with all these human miseries (226).

III

'I DO NOT WISH TO EVER
OFFEND GOD AGAIN'

(*Letters,* volume I, p. 226)

As the soul gradually ascends the mystical ladder, it sees ever more clearly the strident contrast between the infinite holiness and the incomparable perfection of God, and the innate deformity and wickedness of the creatures.

But not only this: it sees with great clarity that, without the full and loving possession of the divine Goodness, the human person will never be able to reach true happiness, being continually threatened by its own unfaithfulness and treachery, that is, by sin.

On the other hand, the vehement desire to attain that complete and definitive possession of the divine Goodness and the legitimate fear of losing it for ever, make the loving soul feel an implacable hatred of sin and declare a fight to the death against it, under all its forms and manifestations.

The soul understands well what sin means and what it signifies in the project of salvation. The soul weeps bitterly on account of sin, and commits itself with great generosity to removing it from itself and from others. It desires to become the lightning rod of offended divine Justice, and offers itself in a surge of love to God as an expiatory victim for sin. The zeal to bring salvation to souls here finds one of its deepest roots.

The fundamental motives of Padre Pio's attitude to sin are all true, profound, theological and supernatural. Notwithstanding this, as often happens to holy souls in the period of the purification of the spirit, Padre Pio uses expressions and phrases which can give a dark and pessimistic impression of what constitutes the normal state of affairs between God and the soul. In the passages that follow Padre Pio presents us with an 'X-ray' of the soul: an image which consists of stark tones of black, grey and white. To come to a clearer understanding of the intense realism of this 'X-ray', it is necessary to illuminate the image it provides with the light of a knowledge that progressively matures in the ways of the Lord: a knowledge that is open to shades of meaning and informs us with ever-growing accuracy of divine holiness and human unworthiness, and of virtue and sin.

⁂

48 When the soul groans and fears to offend God, it does not offend him and it is far from doing so (1011).

49 Regarding the fear you still have of filling the Highest Truth with indignation at your actions, and his justice either by excess or defect, I beg you not to give this any importance. Whoever fears to offend God in truth does not offend him, but rather offends him when this fear ceases (1121).

50 The thought that at any moment I could lose Jesus, causes an anxiety within me that I don't know how to explain; only the soul which loves Jesus sincerely will be able to understand what I mean (328).

51 There is no need to fool ourselves, the enemy is very strong if he does not wish to yield. The soul understands, by the light that God infuses into it, all the danger it is in, if it isn't always on the alert. The thought of losing the All through a possible fall makes the poor soul tremble like a reed exposed to the wind (576).

52 How much I suffer, my Father, when I see that Jesus is not only not cared for by people, but, what is worse, is even affronted, and more than everything with those horrendous blasphemies. I wish I could die or at least become deaf, rather than hear the many affronts that human beings give to God.

I have made the following prayer to God: Lord, let me die rather than letting me find myself with anyone who is in the act of offending you!

Commend me to the Lord, and ask him for this grace for me, if it is for his greater glory (231).

53 For some time now I have felt a need in me to offer myself to the Lord as a victim for poor sinners and souls in purification. This desire has continually grown in my heart so that now it has become, I would say, a strong passion. I have made, it is true, this offer many times to the Lord, begging him to pour over me all the chastisements that are prepared for sinners and souls in purification. The Lord can even increase them a hundredfold for me, so that he might save sinners and admit the souls in purgatory into paradise quickly. But I want to make this offering in obedience. It seems to me that Jesus does want it. I am sure that you will have no difficulty in granting me this permission (206).

54 O God, if everyone knew your severity, just like they knew your sweetness, which creature would be so foolish as to dare to offend you? My God, you, who are very just and very good, show the severity of your justice to all those who dare to offend you, so that they might learn, if not to love you, at least to fear you (477).

55 If you were to perceive that my soul was in danger, you should help me if you didn't want me reduced to the ashes of sin, because I want to save my soul at any cost, and I do not want to offend God any more (226).

56 My Father, I return to you to repeat that I would prefer to die a thousand times rather than allow myself to offend a God who is so good. I would be willing, if it were within my power, to tie all my evil inclinations in one bundle, and hand them to Jesus so that he can burn them all with the fire of his divine love (187).

57 But may the mercy of Jesus live for ever! My confessor assures me that I have sinned venially at most; but what does that matter to me, if this means that I have made Jesus weep? And if the offences committed by every faithful Christian displease him greatly, the offences committed by a priest must displease him so much more. I tell Jesus that I do not wish to commit any more sins; but if he does not support me in my weakness, at the first occasion I will in fact demonstrate to him what I have always been. I have told him that I will love him always; but you know how much I am inclined to evil. Help me, my Father, to expiate this new offence which I have given to Jesus.

Poor Jesus, from me a new offence! My heart is so hard that it does not know how to be moved as it ought at the thought of the offences I have committed. But I want to repent of all that I know how to repent of and all that I can repent of. Tell Jesus at once that he should not refuse my sorrow.

Even though I hope in Jesus' divine mercy, my Father, I tremble and I tremble very much. That's why I have wept in silence, but the tears have been both tears of sorrow, and at the same time tears of a great joy.

But Jesus himself is always with me, and he is not ashamed to still be there, since he continues to reveal himself to me with all the splendours of his heart, with the marvellous expanding of his fatherly love (236).

58 We always walk cautiously, but with holy liberty. We feel that the Lord, who has chained us to himself with love, enables us to look on sin as on a venemous asp; and for the sake of a greater interest we never commit a venial sin deliberately; and as for a mortal sin, we fear it more than fire (407).

59 It is true that my prayers are worthy rather of punishment than reward, because I have sickened Jesus too much by my numberless sins. But in the end he will have pity on me by taking me from the world and calling me to himself, or by freeing me from it. And if neither of these two graces be granted to me, I hope at least that the grace of not giving into temptation may be granted.

Jesus did not measure out the blood that he shed for our salvation, does he want to measure my sins and thus lose me? I think not. He will be revenged quickly and with holiness on this most ungracious of his creatures by means of his holy love.

And what do you say about this? You should say the same, 'I will keep the promise to dismay him no more; and I will strive rather to always love him' (209).

60 I know clearly that if there is in me any good, it has all come from these supernatural goods. I recognise that from this source comes that most ardent determination to suffer all with resignation and readiness, without ever tiring of suffering – even though, alas! with how many imperfections would I do it. I have a most firm resolution not to offend God, not even venially, and I would die a death by fire a thousand times before consciously committing any sin (422).

61 It is true that a life of many centuries spent in the acquisition of eternal glory would count as nothing; but for a soul that fears in every instant to offend God, a day, a single hour, is an infinity (649).

62 To my physical weakness are added the severe struggles of the spirit. The darkest clouds continue to gather in the sky of my poor soul. Jesus is with me, it is true, but how painful, my Father, is the trial that exposes the soul to the risk of offending the divine spouse! But may God live for ever! My trust that I will conquer and be victorious, and the strength to fight on, do not lessen (493).

63 In my present state, in which the merciful God in his infinite wisdom and justice has decided to lift the veil and show me my hidden faults in all their evilness and ugliness, I see myself as so disfigured

that my own clothing seems to be horrified by my vileness.

This has happened to me because the dark picture of my hidden faults that I am viewing has not been created by human hands – if this were so, the soul could easily depict itself as free from blame – but by God, who at this moment executes the work a little in the manner of a judge who allows no appeal.

In this state no creature, neither human nor angelic, is able to place itself between the poor soul and God the Judge, the one who has produced the dark picture. Oh! the happy days of my life, when my most sweet Good was with me and lived inside my heart, where have they gone? I am weary of life. O God, leave the way free for me to lament the bitterness of my heart! O most clement Father, I do not wish to remember now, the faults of my youth that you have already forgotten! Ah! let me weep, my God, over my iniquities. It would have been much better for me if I had perished in my mother's womb before any human eye had seen me (470).

64 Come down with me, Father, into the secret parts of my soul, full of so much imperfection and misery. I am not able to reveal them, but they are numberless. So they seem to me, and they would certainly be repugnant to another person if they were to be described, and would seem to constitute a rejection of the God of purity.

I find nothing that might lessen the just anger of God, unless one can please his Heart, and I cannot find the way to do this. I see that all I have collected for him and given to him have been thorns. This is not merely my opinion, reality shines out in all its clarity. I try to find a way out of this sorrowful state, but I am overcome by that evil which I do not wish to do, without knowing it and without wishing it. Ah! where can I hide from the thunderbolts of a God who thunders and strikes?... But enough of my crying out. It is good for those to keep quiet, who have the duty to keep quiet and who are already completely overcome (1063).

65 Am I not perhaps the most unfortunate of all men? I feel the Lord's hand lie too heavily on me, and it is getting steadily heavier. This I deserve; my iniquities have made the measure run over. But I hope that he who has shown such mercy towards me until now will continue to be merciful on me (482).

66 Alas, my Father, what will become of us when we will appear before this God-Judge of ours and are asked to account for our actions! If such terror is experienced now, through a simple lifting of the veil that had hidden our faults from our eyes so that we might wonder at their ugliness, what will become of us when we must appear before God to bear his severe gaze? (477).

67 Each of my soul's shortcomings, tiny as it maybe, is like a sword of pain that pierces my heart (383).

68 I have a fear, which penetrates right into the deepest part of my spirit and crushes all my bones, of offending even *in minimis* that God who rejects me and persecutes me always and everywhere. This fear I have, even though I see clearly that I will never see this same God seated as absolute monarch at the centre of my heart (767).

69 God knows very well the reason he allows his elect to fall like this. If the only benefit from this were the mortification of my soul, that would be a great thing (915).

70 I am writing to you again to tell you that I continually ask for many graces for your soul in my prayers and in the holy Mass, but I ask especially for the holy and divine love: it is everything for us, it is our honey, my dear Father, in which and with which all our affections, actions and sufferings must be sweetened.

My God, my good Father! How happy is the internal kingdom when his holy love reigns there! How blessed are the powers of our souls when they obey so wise a king! He does not allow grave sins to dwell in the land under his obedience, in his own state, nor any affection for the lightest of sins.

It is true that he does many times allow sins to berth on the frontiers of this land; but this is done in order to train the land's virtues in war and make them courageous. He also allows spies, which are venial sins and imperfections, to move about here and there in his kingdom; but this he allows only to make us realise that without him we would fall prey to our enemies (917).

71 The fear of offending God once again makes me shiver, racks me with pain and agonises me. I fear my heart, which is unfortunately ignorant of what is truly evil. I am firm in my purpose and I resist being influenced by anything I am unsure of; but I fear some surprise move from my heart, that it will allow itself to be dragged along without my depressed will knowing anything of its change. Because

of this I suffer a 'death sentence' fearing that I might have transgressed the command of obedience, or have displeased my God, even in the slightest way (1038).

72 I, however, do not ask to be freed from this tribulation, but I ask that I might be freed from offending God (1257).

73 The thought that I might not be in grace in the eyes of God, the doubt that I might have abused the holy sacraments, that I might not have dealt with holy things in a holy way, that I might not have confessed myself fully and well, is a thorn that continually lacerates my heart. I no longer know to which saint I should dedicate myself or what means to use (1255).

74 I do not ask Jesus to remove this tribulation, no; I only ask not to offend him and I ask a little light to understand whether this be a punishment for my unfaithfulness (1267).

75 Not knowing whether one works for the glory of God or gives him offence, is more painful than death itself (839).

76 My Father, how hard is it to undergo a trial where there is no glimmer of light or comfort! If one could at least know that everything was working for the glory of God! If only I knew that this is the case, then even hell on this earth would be very sweet to me. But may the will of God be done (822).

77 There has been no let-up at all in the furious battle. It follows its regular path, of course, but

pursues me and always marches forward. My God, when will I be able to rest awhile peacefully in you? When will this nail at least be removed, which breaks my heart and makes a hole in my head, so that I might know that in all this hell I do not offend you? My God, I would be ready to suffer a thousand hells of this type, as long as a glimmer of your light would enter my mind and confirm that in all of this I do in fact love you! (1260).

78 Who could, my Father, lay bare the tremendous miseries of my spirit? I feel that I die in every instant; I seem to vacillate in every moment, and yet I would suffer death an infinite number of times before offending God with open eyes (817).

79 What alone grieves me, in certain moments, is not being certain if, at the first assault of the enemy I was ready to resist him. I believe, on examining myself now, that I would prefer death rather than intentionally offend my dear Jesus... even a single sin, however light (196).

80 But I cannot understand how these fears and discomforts can exist in a heart that would prefer to die rather than to sin deliberately... Amidst these tortures which my heart suffers I feel a greater trust in God, and I am so full of my sins that I endure moments of continual torment.

The only comfort that remains to me in the midst of this sorrow, which I would call almost infinite, is to weep; weeping offers me both comfort and relief (186).

81 May your faith again illuminate my intellect, your charity warm this heart shattered by the sorrow of offending you in the hour of trial (838).

82 My whole person is consecrated to Jesus and I feel myself bound to him by a double bond, as a Christian and as a Priest. For precisely this reason I tremble at the mere thought that this double bond might be loosened at any moment.

Could such a bond be broken, or, what is worse, could it ever be broken without one's knowing it – whilst being certain even that it remains unbroken, with a certainty akin to that of God's existence? I feel the depths of my spirit answer that this could never happen, unless one became something awful, like the originator of heresy (498).

IV

'I SUFFER AND I WISH ALWAYS TO SUFFER MORE'

(*Letters*, volume I, p. 357)

Padre Pio was undoubtedly a victim of sorrow and followed the sorrowful way of Calvary step by step. The sorrowful dimension of his Spiritual journey contains many disturbing events and is described using phrases of a disconcertingly dramatic nature. The intense and varied sorrow that is revealed in his actions and words has a transcendent value. This sorrow is an integral and indispensable part of the 'great mission' entrusted to him by God, and his personal part in the completion of Jesus' passion.

In order to carry out the task that was entrusted to him in the 'vocation to co-redeem', he offered himself as a victim of love and expiation, and lived continually as a victim, accepting with generosity and without reserve the painful consequences of the offer that he had freely made. Consequently, the sorrow which he desired with ardour, accepted with love and suffered with generosity, became his atmosphere and the air he breathed. To be deprived of it would have been his greatest torment, and life impossible without it.

The experiences and teachings that are witnessed to in the following passages, chosen from among many, can be understood and their true value appreciated only by someone who meditates on them in the shadow of the Cross. It was the Cross that illuminated all Padre Pio's life and it was the Cross that sustained him in all his battles. Ultimately, these sentences were inspired by, and the experiences brought about by, God's redeeming blood; they were made fruitful and sanctifying by Padre Pio's generous and loving participation in the sorrows of Jesus.

The reader will find in these letters numerous cornerstones for the construction of a theology of suffering taught by practice rather than theory.

⚜

83 I know with certainty that I feel a most burning thirst to suffer very much, and I feel a continual need to say to the Lord without interruption: '*Aut pati aut mori*', or rather: '*Semper pati et nunquam mori*'[8] (627).

84 I know that you suffer because I am not near and you cannot help me. But rejoice, my Father, because I am more happy than ever in my suffering, and if I didn't listen to my heart, I would ask Jesus to give me all the sadness of humankind; but I don't, because I fear that I might become too selfish, thirsting after the better part: suffering. Jesus is closer to us when we suffer; he watches over us, it is he who comes to beg suffering, tears… and he needs them to help souls (270).

---

8. ' "Either to suffer or to die", or rather: "Always to suffer and never die" '.

85 Do not forget that I am a selfish person when it comes to suffering; I want only to suffer and, while I am impatient to leave this life for Jesus' company, I would reproach myself if I tried – even for an hour – to be left without a cross, or even worse, if others were to come and take it from me (304).

86 I am experiencing such a strange solitude that neither all the creatures here below, nor the very inhabitants of heaven, unless my Beloved was also there, would be able to keep me company. In this world I can find no relief; everything wearies me and torments me. But I want to suffer all these tortures for my whole life, if this agony of my soul pleases God, in spite of the fact that I know myself and my weaknesses (367).

87 My shame is great when I see myself so unworthy of such a favour. I would like to have an infinite number of lives so that I could use them for God, and at that very moment I complain vigorously to Jesus because he offers me few opportunities to suffer (368).

88 The other effect of this grace is that my life is becoming a cruel martyrdom. The only comfort I have lies in my resignation to live for the love of Jesus. But alas! my Father, even in this comfort there is a pain that in certain moments is unbearable, because my soul wishes that my entire life were sowed with crosses and persecutions (383).

89 Jesus, when he wants me to know that he loves me, lets me taste the sores, the thorns, the agony of his Passion… When he wants to make me rejoice,

he fills my heart with that spirit which is all fire; he talks to me about his suffering; he invites me, with a voice that is both a plea and a command, to lend my body to lighten his sorrows (335).

90 Jesus alone understands how much I suffer when he brings me before the sorrowful scene of Calvary. Equally incomprehensible is the relief that one gives to Jesus, not only in suffering with him in his sorrow, but when he finds a soul that for love of him does not ask for consolations, but to be allowed to participate in these very sorrows (335).

91 I want nobody, but Jesus alone; I desire nothing else than suffering from him (which is Jesus' own desire). Let me say it, because no one can overhear us in this letter: I am prepared to be deprived forever of the sweetness that Jesus makes me experience, I am ready to suffer Jesus' hiding of his beautiful eyes from me, as long as he doesn't hide his love, which would kill me. But to be deprived of suffering, I am not able, I do not have the strength (335).

92 Perhaps I still haven't expressed myself clearly regarding the secret of this suffering. Jesus, Man of Sorrows, desires that all Christians imitate him. Now Jesus has offered this chalice to me; I have accepted it, which is why he doesn't spare me it. My poor suffering is worth nothing, but Jesus is still pleased with it, because on the earth he greatly loved suffering. Therefore, on certain days when he suffers greatly on this earth, he allows me to feel the suffering even more.

Now shouldn't this only serve to humble me and spur me to hide myself from the eyes of all people, because I have been made worthy to suffer with Jesus and as Jesus? Ah, my Father, I feel that my ingratitude to the majesty of God is in fact far too great! (335).

93 Tuesday and Thursday evening to Saturday, was a sorrowful tragedy. My heart, my hands and my feet seemed to have been pierced by a sword; so great is the pain that I feel (266).

94 Even in my physical state I feel very bad, so much so that I have spent some days in bed. But I rejoice in all of this and it seems that I keep a joyful and resigned soul, because I remember with pleasure the sacrifice of my life which I have made to the Lord. And if it were not for the Spiritual afflictions that tear my heart, I would almost be in a paradise of delights. But may the will of God be done (278).

95 May the hand of our dear Jesus be blessed; the hand that strikes me and makes me worthy, against all my merits, to suffer something for his love and through this suffering allows me to make satisfaction for my many faults! (187).

96 I want to suffer. This is my longing. May it be given to me to know how to suffer and go in peace to my own defeat, with the abandonment of God, to the just and worthy punishment of my unfaithfulness (1051).

97 I desire death only to unite me with indissoluble bonds to the heavenly Spouse. I desire life also so that I can always suffer more, because Jesus has given me to understand that suffering is the only sure test of love. It seems to me that I am always looking for something that I do not find; neither do I know

what this thing is that I continually search for: I love, I suffer little; I want to love this thing that I search for very much more; I want to suffer very much more for this ideal that I am searching for (358).

98 A very great pleasure fills all my heart, it makes me blessed and happy: I suffer, and want to suffer without interruption; I feel myself consumed, and want to be consumed without ceasing (357).

99 You must believe me, my Father, that I can find happiness in these sufferings. Jesus himself wants my sufferings, he needs them for the good of souls. But I ask myself: what relief can I give him with my sufferings? What a destiny! O to what a height the most sweet Jesus has raised my soul! (307).

100 He [God] chooses some souls. From among these, despite all my faults, he has also chosen my soul to help him in the great project of saving humanity. The more these chosen souls suffer without any comfort, the more the sufferings of our good Jesus are lightened.

Well, that's the reason why I wish to suffer unceasingly, and to suffer without comfort; and from this I derive all my joy. This I can testify to through the long experience I have had of it, provided that one does not cease to cry out to him (304).

101 When will the Lord desire to remove from you completely the cross he has given you? I pray for this always. I renew continually the offer made to Jesus for you. What more must I do? You yourself must offer me to Jesus, so that he can make you happy. You must not stop yourself doing it when

you think of my weakness. Jesus will help me! Besides the present sacrifice, which I always renew, I am utterly ready to make hundreds more, even the most painful (808).

102 I feel in my heart the urgent need to cry out ever more strongly to Jesus with St Augustine, the Doctor of Grace: '*Da quod iubes, et iube quod vis.*'[9] Therefore, my dear Father, don't let the thought of my suffering place any sort of shadow on your brow or in your eyes, that might sadden your heart. Yes, let us not weep, my dearest Father; we should hide our tears from the one who sends them, from he who has shed, and who sheds every day, many of his own on account of the ingratitude of humankind (303).

103 All the ugly spectres that the devil is introducing into my mind, disappear when, trusting, I abandon myself into the arms of Jesus. Therefore if I am with Jesus Crucified, that is, when I meditate on his troubles, I suffer immensely, but it is a suffering that does me a lot of good. I enjoy a peace and tranquillity which cannot be explained (217).

104 Patience!… I suffer, it is true, but I greatly rejoice in my suffering, you yourself having assured me that it does not mean that I am abandoned by God, but is an expression of how thoughtful his love is. I hope that the Lord will accept my sufferings in satisfaction for the numerous offences that I have given him. In short, all my suffering is nothing compared to what I deserve for my sins (206).

---

9. Augustine, *Confessions* X, 29,40: 'Give what you command, and command what you will.'

105 My heart overflows with joy, and I feel myself ever more capable of meeting any affliction, whatever it is that pleases Jesus (196).

106 Alas, I feel that sharp pain within my spirit, the thorn that agonises me day and night! What bitter pain I experience in my extremities and in my heart! All these pains keep me in a continual swoon, and however sweet this swoon may be, it is equally painful and sharp.

In the midst of so much torture, both loving and painful at the same time, two conflicting feelings are true: one which wants to reject the suffering, and the other which desires it. And the mere thought of living for a time without this intense and loving martyrdom, terrifies me, frightens me, agonises me (1103).

107 'My son,' said Jesus, 'I need victims to calm the just, divine, anger of my Father; renew the sacrifice of your entire self to me, and do it without any reservation.'

My Father, I renewed the sacrifice of my life to him, and if I feel in myself a sense of sadness, it comes from contemplating the God of suffering. If you can, try to find souls that offer themselves to the Lord as victims for sinners. Jesus will help you (343).

108 Didn't I tell you that Jesus wants me to suffer without any comfort? Didn't he ask me, and elect me, to be one of his victims. I must journey on, dear Father, to the *consummatum est* and the *in manus tuas*[10] (310).

---

10. 'It is finished' (Jn 19:30) and the 'Into your hands' (Lk 23:46).

109 Jesus, his beloved Mother, my Guardian Angel and others are encouraging me, not neglecting to repeat that anyone who calls themselves a victim must lose all their blood. It is sweet and consoling to fight with such a tender Father alongside (314).

110 Let us always contemplate with the eye of faith, which is our pious and loving angel, Jesus Christ ascending Calvary carrying his cross. And as he conquers the steep slope at great cost, we see him followed by an immense crowd of souls who close to him carry their own crosses and follow the same path (597).

111 Oh, how beautiful this sight is [of the immense crowd of souls who close to him carry their own crosses]! Let us fix the mind's eye well on this sight. We can see our most holy Mother right next to Jesus, she who follows Jesus in complete perfection, weighed down by her own cross. Then follow the apostles, the martyrs, the doctors of the Church, the virgins, the confessors. Oh, how holy, noble, august, worthy and dear this company is! Oh, in it, how joy is sincere, peace profound, the step courageous, the life perfect! Faith animates the company, trust sustains it, charity ignites it, modesty beautifies it, penitence adorns it (597).

112 In this company all consolations are united to all sacrifices, all hope to all virtues. Who will grant us to belong to such a fine company? But long live God! Jesus, despite our unworthiness, has placed us in such a fine company. Let us strive to belong to their ranks more and more, and let us hurry to walk the way of Calvary with them; let us look to the end of our journey; let us not leave this fine company; let us refuse any way that is not the way taken by it (598).

113 Let us keep our gaze fixed on this noble, august and holy company that follows Jesus to Golgotha. There is not one of them that does not bear the profession of the true faith on their forehead, renunciation in the heart and the cross on their shoulders. Let us take courage and follow this adventurous people, in which all consolations are joined to all sacrifices, all hope to all virtues (603).

114 Long live Jesus who wants me in this way, despite all my unworthiness, to enter into some of his suffering! Oh! how unbearable, my Father, is the pain suffered far from the cross! But how it becomes sweet and bearable if one offers it near the Cross of Jesus! All becomes easy for the soul, even though the soul feels itself oppressed and drunk with every sort of suffering. Deep down, in its depths, the soul has a holy fear that it might fall and sicken the divine Spouse; if it were not for this fear, the soul would feel itself to be in paradise, so great is the sweetness that this way of suffering brings it.

The soul placed in such a state – Oh! how many times – in its exultation turns to the divine Master and says: 'Yes, O Jesus, your yoke is truly easy and your burden truly light!' (579).

115 Jesus tells me that in love it is he who delights me; in suffering, on the other hand, it is I who delight him. To wish for health would be to go in search of joys for myself, and not try to comfort

him. Yes, I love the Cross, the Cross alone; I love it because I see it constantly on Jesus' shoulders. Jesus knows very well now that all my life, all my heart are dedicated to him and to his sorrows (335).

116 I do not know what is happening to me. I know one thing only with certainty: the Lord will not break his promises. 'Do not fear, I will make you suffer, but I will give you strength' (Jesus keeps repeating to me). 'I desire that your heart be purified and proved through a hidden, daily martyrdom. Do not be frightened if I allow the devil to torment you, the world to sicken you and all those persons most dear to you to afflict you, because nothing can defeat those who groan beneath the Cross for love of me, and whom I have striven to protect' (339).

117 Yesterday evening [7.9.1911], something happened to me that I can neither explain nor understand. In the middle of my palms there appeared a spot of red almost in the shape of a penny, accompanied by a sharp and strong pain in the spot's centre. This pain was more perceptible in the middle of the left hand, and it's still there. I notice also some pain on the soles of my feet.

For almost a year this phenomenon had been constantly recurring, though not recently. Don't be surprised that this is the first time I'm telling you about it, because I have always before been overcome by a deep sense of shame. If only you knew, even now, how much violence I've had to do to myself to tell you about it! (234).

118 On the morning of the twentieth of last month [September] while in choir, after the

celebration of holy Mass, I was overcome by a sense of repose, like a sweet sleep. All my internal and external senses, as well as the faculties of my soul, found themselves in an indescribable stillness. I felt a total silence descend around me and within me; this was immediately followed by a sense of great peace and of an abandonment to the complete loss of everything, and in the midst of all this some respite. All of this happened in a flash.

And while all this was happening, I saw before me a mysterious person, similar to the one I saw on the fifth of August, different only in that he had hands, feet and side which were pouring with blood.

The sight of him terrified me. I would not know how to tell you what I felt in that instant. I felt myself dying, and I would be dead if the Lord hadn't kept my heart going, which I felt leaping about in my chest.

The vision of this person withdrew, and I noticed that my hands, feet and side were pierced and pouring with blood. Imagine the agony that I felt then, and that I continue to feel almost every day.

The wound of the heart poured constantly with blood, especially from Thursday evening until Saturday. My Father, I am dying of the pain because of this agony and the ensuing shame that I feel deep in my soul. I fear that I will die for loss of blood, if the Lord does not listen to the groans of my poor heart, and to my call for an end to what's happening to me.

Will Jesus, who is so good, do me this grace? Will he at least take from me this shame that I feel on account of these external marks that I bear? I will raise my voice loudly to him and will not cease to implore him, for the sake of his mercy, not to take away the agony, nor the suffering (because seems to me impossible and I want to inebriate myself with suffering), but the marks that shame and humiliate me in an indescribable and unbearable way (1093).

119 I will not cease to raise my hands in the holy place during the night and will bless you always as long as there is breath left in me.

I implore you, O my good God, to be my life, my boat and my port. You have helped me to mount your Son's Cross, and I strive to bear it in the best way possible. I am certain that I will never come down from it and I will never see the sky grow brighter. I am convinced that when we speak to you, we speak among thunders and lightnings; and we see you in the bush's fire and thorns. But to do this we must take our shoes off and entirely renounce our own will and affections.

I am prepared for all of this, but will you show yourself one day on Tabor, during the holy sunset? Will I have the strength tirelessly to ascend to the heavenly vision of my Saviour? I feel the ground on which I walk giving way beneath my feet. Who will make my footsteps firm, if not you, who are the staff of my weakness? Have mercy on me, O God, have mercy on me! Do not let me experience my weakness any more! (837).

120 I suffer, indeed, I suffer greatly, but thanks to the good Jesus I feel a little strength. And what is the creature which is helped by God, not capable of?

I do not at all yearn for my cross to be made lighter, because suffering with Jesus is something I hold very dear. When I contemplate the cross on Jesus' shoulders I always feel strengthened and I exult in a holy joy (303).

121 How many times – Jesus said to me a little while ago – would you have abandoned me, if I hadn't crucified you. Under the Cross one learns to love, and I do not give it to all, only to those souls that are dearest to me (339).

122 But when, my Father, will my exile end? Whether I like it or not, I am resigned to the will of heaven. But let God's plans be fulfilled in me, so that our dear Jesus might be glorified.

In certain moments my soul suffers greatly, and if this agony wasn't interrupted from time to time by moments of respite, who knows what would become of me. Yes, my Father, in the most difficult hour of the trial our merciful Lord comes to my aid and, like the loving Father that he is, consoles me and encourages me to run ever more in the way of the Cross. I do suffer; but I do not become saddened, because Jesus wants it thus (193).

123 In the midst of so much agony, I feel the strength to pronounce the sorrowful *fiat*.[11] Oh *fiat*, how you are both sweet and bitter! You wound and heal, give sores and cure, give both death and life at the same time! O sweet torments, why are you at once so unbearable and so dear? O sweet wounds, why is it that while you are so painful, you soothe the spirit, and at the same time you prepare it to submit itself to the blows of new trials? (1103).

124 Let us keep alight in our hearts the flame of charity and never lose courage. And if some

---

11. 'Let it be done'.

languor or weakness of spirit comes over us, let us run to the foot of the Cross and drown in the heavenly perfumes, and we will be without doubt reinvigorated (918).

125 The heavenly Father does not fail to help me participate in the sufferings of his only-begotten Son, even physically. These sufferings are so acute that they can be neither described nor imagined! I do not know whether it be due to a lack of strength, or if there be some fault when, put in this state, I cry like a child without wanting to (873).

126 I blush: I know very well that the Cross is the pledge of love, the Cross is the deposit for forgiveness, and the love that is not fed and nourished by the Cross is not true love, and becomes fire on straw. And yet even with such knowledge, this false disciple of the Nazarene feels the Cross weigh very heavily on his heart, and many times (do not be scandalised and do not be horrified, O Father, about what I am going to say) goes in search of the merciful one from Cyrene[12] to relieve him and comfort him! What merit can my love have in God's eyes? (571).

127 My Father, I have a very great desire to suffer for the love of Jesus. How is it, then, that when it comes to the test, against my every wish, I search for some relief? I must use much strength and violence against myself in these trials in order to silence nature which, so to speak, cries loudly to be consoled. I do not wish to experience this struggle. Many times

---

12. Lk 23:26.

it makes me cry like a child, because it seems to me that the cause of the struggle is my own lack of love and of likeness to God. What do you think about it? (572).

V

'I LIVE IN A PERPETUAL NIGHT'

(*Letters*, volume I, p. 817)

The dark night of the spirit belongs to the *via dolorosa*, along which Padre Pio travelled, and to the fulfilment of his self-offering as victim in his 'mission of co-redemption'.

The clarity and precision of his ideas when he speaks of the nature and purpose of this mystical process is exceptional, as is the liveliness of the images and expressions with which he describes the principal phases of purification that mark it and the principal factors that determine it.

As would be expected, in the case of Padre Pio we are dealing with painfully lived experiences, rather than conclusions of an in-depth study. But the importance and originality of the themes here addressed will escape no one.

It has not been easy to choose from the many pages that describe this stage in the mystical journey those that seem to be more important. The few that have been chosen, however, will suffice to help us see the crucifying sorrows, the atrocious incubi and the overwhelming griefs that afflict the soul, purify it and prepare it for perfect union with God. In realistic, expressive and impassioned terms, Padre Pio speaks of the agonising desolation of abandonment by God, of the fruitless and prolonged searches for the highest Good, of the desolating recognition of one's own nothingness before God's ineffable holiness.

When faced with the intensity and ceaseless nature of the trial the soul does not abandon its journey; though it is continually wrapped in a dense fog, it turns without fail to the sources of help and support which the Spirit, the instructions of guides and personal experience all make available to it: prayer, faithfulness to promises, conformity to the divine will, submission to authority.

꒰ঌ◦✦◦໒꒱

128 The Lord gives us burdens and he removes them, because when he gives a cross to one of his elect, he so strengthens them that, bearing the weight with this strength, they are relieved of its burden (974).

129 Have courage, therefore, and move forward always. Be comforted, however, O soul, because Jesus' conduct towards you is not because he rejects you but because he wants to attract you to himself, desiring you entirely for himself. He loves you more than you can imagine (780).

130 To souls loved by God, tribulations are more precious than gold or rest. These souls will be very happy if they constantly persevere: 'For a day in your courts is better than a thousand years in the tents of sinners', sang the royal Prophet[13] (967).

131 In the midst of the trials that God's goodness exposes you to, continue, Father, to live entirely in God. What greater happiness is there, Father,

---

13. Ps 84:10.

than to live entirely in God, since he loves his own, he protects them, guides them and leads them to the longed-for harbour of eternity (927).

132 Yes, my God, do not delay in coming to my aid! Do you not see that I have no more strength to fight, that all my vigour is gone? O my God, you who know the extreme bitterness of my spirit, do not delay in coming to my aid. You alone can and must draw me out of this prison of death. Ah! no. I will not grow weary of crying loudly with Job: 'Even though he kills me, I will not cease to hope in him'[14] (1260).

133 I am extremely afflicted because I see myself in such bitterness; but I rejoice when I gaze on the goodness of the Lord, who is showing such favour towards you. Yes, Father, the way the Lord is treating you shows how he favours you. It has nothing to do with abandonment, vengeful justice, or your unworthiness, which itself merits rejection and condemnation. All that happens in you is the result of love, of God's great love for you; it is a most loving trial that God gives to his elect; it is a vocation to co-redeem, and is therefore a source of glory.

If we accept this as certain and beyond doubt, then all the anxieties and trepidations that the enemy causes to arise, will collapse. The enemy takes an evil pleasure in tormenting us and the highest Good permits this to happen, always with the aim that we mentioned above. You should laugh at these doubts and perplexities, because they come from Satan (1209).

---

14. Job 13:15.

134 My God! my Father! truly this state is unbearable, painful, desolate and almost unsustainable. One cannot describe the state in which my soul finds itself. In certain moments, if it wasn't for divine grace supporting me, I would be on the point of death and almost in despair. Only submission to the divine will gives me a little peace.

But then the eye lowers itself again onto one's own brothers, who encircle one, and once again the bitterness returns. The soul, in so far as it sees itself reflected in God, experiences the greatest sweetness; in so far as it sees itself reflected in one's neighbour, it experiences the greatest bitterness.

And between these two extremes I feel myself dying, I agonise without ever dying. Alas! I am the most unhappy of creatures! Who will rescue me from this living death, from these two opposing extremes that tyrannise me and devour me? (1153).

135 'I am in the habit of using repeated blows with a salutary chisel and meticulous cleaning to prepare the stones that must form part of the eternal edifice.' Every time he gifts me with new crosses, Jesus repeats these words (329).

136 May he make a little heavenly dew to descend into the hearts of those afflicted souls! ... God has plunged their intellects into darkness, placed their will in aridity, their memories in emptiness, their hearts in bitterness, despondency and a great desolation. And all of this is most enviable, because it all helps our hearts to dispose and prepare themselves to receive the true Spirit, which is nothing other than the union of love (440).

137 God is with them [souls], and this should be enough to persuade them always to be ready to dedicate themselves totally to God, and to perform works for his service and honour. They shouldn't take notice of the fact that this will to dedicate themselves to God and to perform works to the glory and honour of his majesty, once produced in them a certain sweet and gentle effect, both in their spirit and in their sensitive appetites. These pleasant effects not being essential, God concedes it to weak souls which are still children in the spirit, but takes it from the souls already strengthened in spirit (440).

138 In order to ascend to divine contemplation, the soul must be purified of all its imperfections, and not only those it presently has – which one attains through the purgation of the senses – but also from all its habitual imperfections. Such habitual imperfections, like certain attachments and habits of imperfection, cannot be eradicated through the purgation of the senses and their roots remain in the soul – purification from these is attained through the purgation of the spirit, with which God penetrates the soul to its core with a most rarefied light, inwardly transfixes it and completely renews it (441).

139 This most rarefied light, which God causes to descend into the said souls, lays siege to them in a most desolate and purgative manner, causing the greatest and death-like afflictions and interior pains. These souls cannot at this time comprehend this divine working, this most rarefied light. This is so for two reasons: the first is that, due to its nature – it being so lofty, so sublime – this light completely surpasses the capacity of their souls and becomes rather a cause of

darkness and torment than light. The second reason is the baseness and impurity of the souls themselves, which means that the rarefied light not only becomes dark to them but also painful, and it afflicts them. Thus, instead of consoling them, it grieves them, filling them with great pain on the level of their sensitive appetites, and causing their Spiritual powers to feel great anxiety and horrendous pains.

All this happens in the beginning, when the divine light has found the souls averse to divine union and therefore deals with them in a purgative way. And when this light has purged them, it deals with them in an illuminative way, raising them to the vision and perfect union with God (441).

140 *'Quare posuisti me contrarium tibi, et factus sum mihimetipsi gravis?'*[15] So cries my soul from the depths of the wretchedness in which its God has placed it. My soul has been placed by the Lord to waste away in suffering. My state is bitter, it is terrible and it is extremely frightening. All is dark, around me and within me: darkness in the intellect, distress in the will, I am troubled in the memory. The thought of faith alone keeps me standing: on the inside I am suffering, and at the same time I am afflicted by, and longing for, the divine love.

Is this state I am in a grace, or does it indicate eternal abandonment, God's eternal withdrawal from me, on account of the continual indignation that my life causes to him? Will my spirit find in God a loving Father who always welcomes it, or a severe Judge who will condemn it? I am not in a position to know this.

---

15. Job 7:20: 'Why have you made me your target? Why have I become a burden to you?'.

O terrible darkness! O terrible uncertainty! I am almost unable to stand it any longer: the hand of God lies more heavily upon me. To die would be a relief.

In this state, it torments me especially to see that I am not worthy of God, and I never will be, because I see my ugliness plainly and clearly. I know also, in the clearest possible way, that I am completely unworthy of God, and of any creature. My soul sees lining up before it, one by one, all those evils by which it made itself guilty before God; and in this line-up it sees with its own eyes things which it will never have again.

Now the soul understands what the royal Prophet said: 'You correct man for iniquity, and you make his soul waste away like a spider (that disembowels itself)'; '*propter iniquitatem corripuisti hominem et tabescere fecisti sicut araneam animam eius*'.[16] But this fortunate man whom the prophet is speaking about is accepted by God, and what he experiences is God's merciful touch giving him new favours, not bringing punishment. If only God wanted it to be so for me also!

Affected by this thought, and this burden, my soul is so distant from thinking that it is favoured by God, that it seems the minimal amount of support that remained has now disappeared along with everything else, and there is not a single soul able to pity it.

Most pitiable state that fills me full of the greatest confusion! I would like to hide from God's eyes, and from the eyes of all his creatures. I would like to hide from myself, so great is the pain that my wretchedness, my imperfection, my poverty causes me that they drown my whole spirit in darkness.

---

16. Ps 37:12.

But Father, I myself cannot describe to you my present state. If you want a brief description of my entire interior state, pause a little and consider what the prophet Jonah says of himself, for exactly the same can be said of my own state: 'You cast me into the deep, into the heart of the seas, and the flood surrounded me; all your waves and your billows passed over me. Then I said, "I am driven away from your sight; but will I yet see your holy temple?"' (note, Father, that neither in my case has all hope disappeared). 'The waters closed in over me; the deep surrounded me; weeds were wrapped around my head I descended to the roots of the mountains. I went down to the land whose bars closed upon me forever.'[17]

Have a look, as well, at what the royal Prophet says of himself: 'Save me, O God, for the waters have come up to my soul. I sink in deep mire, where there is no foothold; I have tried to right myself in the sea, and the flood sweeps over me. I am weary with my crying; my throat is parched. My eyes grow dim with waiting for my God.'[18]

Behold, O Father, the faithful expressions of my deplorable state, expressed so exactly by those two great saints of the first covenant. My suffering is most agonising, and can only be compared to the pains of someone who is denied any air and unable to breathe.

Oh! God forbid that you should find this comparison exaggerated. I must add, in honour of the truth, that it is rather pale when compared to the suffering I experience. In truth, I am full of sorrow and there is not one part of me that is not deeply

---

17. Jonah 2:3-6.
18. Ps 69:1-3.

distressed: the sensitive part is in a bitter and terrible aridity; the powers of the soul are all empty of all their apprehensions, and this fills me with the greatest fear.

The spirit lies in the black darkness and the body itself is not excluded from all these sufferings. The pain, even though it is not physical but entirely spiritual, doesn't allow the body to escape participation, and it participates to a high degree, in a way that is completely new and unknown. In this state there arises such pain between the soul and body that it is impossible for me to give an illustration of it. But long live God! If these sufferings weren't tempered at God's command by his orders, they being the greatest when I am at my strongest, my life would unravel in a very short time. But the deepest bitterness is experienced only in small doses.

In certain instants, my Father, it is so awful that the soul seems to see hell and eternal damnation open up beneath its feet. Alas! who will free me from all this misfortune? Who will sustain me? Who will remember me in my poverty, my excesses, my bitterness and my rancour?

God's fury, O Father, is certainly upon me, and all his waves, as the prophet says, have overwhelmed me.[19] God has distanced from me my friends and those I know, and all hold me in abhorrence. I do nothing but struggle and weep by day and night. The Father Provincial, in whom I confided regarding my current state, enjoined complete silence on me and I don't know why; my confessor rebukes me, and I find no comfort in his long homilies on this subject. He has much to say when he explains about all the causes for

---

19. Ps 88:7.

comfort there are, and how I must hold onto them; he speaks well of all the good things that these evils are producing in my soul, enumerating them one by one. I am not able to calm myself, and I am unable to believe him. This is because I am totally soaked and immersed in all the experience of my evils, and I see clearly all my many miseries; and, on the other hand, I know that he doesn't see them or feel them as my own soul feels and sees them, which means I know for myself that not all he says applies to me.

And so, my dear Father, instead of consolation I receive greater torment. As you see, I climb the summit of Calvary on my own, deprived of every heavenly and every human comfort. If I could at least pray or cry out! It seems that Jesus rejects my prayer: he threatens me and drags me around in the darkness, and not towards the light.

He reveals all my poverty under the rod of his indignation. His hand lies continually on me, and this hand is so heavy and unbearable that, as Jeremiah says, 'He has made my flesh and my skin waste away, and broken my bones.'[20]

Oh! how heavy this divine hand is, my Father; a hand that is, when all things are considered, still the hand of a loving Father! What will this hand be for those unfortunate ones, for those who find themselves in hell?

I plead, but his hand always pushes me away: he confines me to the darkness, like the everlasting dead. His hand is raising a building about me, which surrounds me with bitterness and weariness. His hand can no longer be endured; it squeezes me ever more tightly in its shackles.

---

20. Lam 3:4.

This blessed hand turns everything upside down, it crushes everything and leaves me utterly desolate. What does the Lord want to do with me? Will the outcome of my days be in the Lord's ways? And as I raise my humble prayer to God from the bottom of my heart: '*nolo multa fortitudine contendat mecum nec magnitudinis suae male me premat*',[21] I turn also to you so that you might in all sincerity and frankness talk to me in the Lord.

Tell me frankly, I am ready for anything, can I still hope for salvation from the mercy of the Lord? What have I ever done to call such misfortune down on me? Will my soul yet sing a song of victory, or will it have to tell forever of the vigours of God's justice it experiences. Is it possible that I love God?

Listen, Father, amongst all the torments that make my soul waste away, the first place is occupied by the unremitting grief or worry caused by the thought of God, which leads me to suppose that I do not love him or truly serve him (612).

141 I desire that my mind should think only of Jesus, my heart beat only and always for him; and all of this I promise Jesus assiduously. But alas! I realise very well that my mind wanders, or better, is tried very sorely, and that the spirit, too, becomes thus affected, and the heart can do nothing but waste away in sorrow. It is true, of course, that I am wholly consecrated to Jesus and I intend to suffer all this for him – but I am not able to convince myself of this (873).

---

21. Job 23:6: 'I would that he did not contend with me with great power, so that he might not oppress me with the greatness of his majesty.'

142 I do not feel physically very well, but what should I say to you about how I feel morally? My Father, the night becomes ever more deep; the storm ever more severe; the struggle ever more pressing, and all threatens to submerge the poor little boat of my spirit.

No comfort descends into my soul. I have become completely blind. All that I can see clearly – if one can speak about sight in this case – is my nothingness, on one hand, and on the other, the goodness and greatness of God. I see God within me, but this is far from satisfying my longing, because I feel a greater desire for him. I see God surrounded by a thick fog, and this fog gets increasingly thicker with the passing of the days. Alas, when will he be revealed to my gaze? When will the divine Sun shine out in me? Can and should I hope to see this sun, or will I have to remain eternally immersed in this pitch darkness? (821).

143 I am being put to the test in everything. I live in a perpetual night, and there is no sign at all that its thick darkness will give way to the beautiful dawn. I feel God in the centre of my soul, but I don't know how to tell you how I feel this. His presence, far from consoling me, infinitely increases my torment, which in every instant causes me to fall into an extremely painful swoon. I feel that he is present to me now; and yet how his presence is covered in a fog! My gaze is fixed continually on this strange and mysterious presence, and the more I fix my gaze the more I feel my interior sorrow grow, because the object of my contemplation grows itself ever larger and renders itself ever more hidden (817).

144 I feel my heart break on account of the sorrow, and I have nowhere to put it. I feel, and I carry, death in my heart. I long greatly to see the light, but the more this longing grows the thicker and more frightening the darkness becomes. And in this hellish chaos I hear and see nothing but the roaring of bloodthirsty lions, that are ever ready to devour their prey (996).

145 But *fiat*, I repeat always; and I long for nothing other than the fulfilment of this *fiat* in exactly the way the Lord requests – with generosity and strength. Ah! Father, I beg your diligent help in prayer, because I see myself on the very point of being crushed, suffocated and drowned beneath such a hard trial. I see hell open up beneath my feet, or better, I've already descended into it. I am on the point of shipwreck (1038).

146 I, too, have been in bed with the Spanish fever, which is causing deaths here also. How desirable it would have been for the Lord to call me to himself! But he has reduced me to a most wretched existence because of the struggles I endure.

I have spent, and spend, hours that are terrible and sorrowful. They think me dead at every turn, both physically and morally. God is unknown to my spirit! O Good of my soul, where are you? Where have you hidden yourself? Do you not see, Jesus, that my soul wants to see you at any price? It seeks you in every place, but you allow yourself to be found only in the fullness of your fury where you fill it with the greatest disturbance and bitterness, leading it to believe how much it belongs to you. Who could express the seriousness of my position? All the things that are clear to me when reflected in your light, I am unable to express in human language. And when I want to stammer something out, the soul thinks it has erred and that it is more than ever distant from the truth of the matter.

My Good! are you lost to me forever? I desire to cry out and lament at the top of my voice, but I am very weak and my strength has deserted me. And what will I ever be able to achieve if I'm not able to make my lament ascend to your throne: 'My God, my God, why have you abandoned me?'[22]

My soul is totally preoccupied with the clear picture of my wretchedness! My God, how can I stand such a sorrowful sight! Withdraw your light that reveals to me what I am, because I am not able to withstand the clear contrast it presents to me! My Father, in the light of God's splendour I see all my own wickedness and ingratitude. I see the bad old man, crouched inside myself, he seems to want to repay God tit for tat for being absent, denying God his rights; the very rights that constitute some of this old man's strictest duties. And what strength it requires to get him up onto his feet! My God! Come quickly to my aid, because I fear for myself, faithless and ungrateful creature; protect me from my powerful enemies!

I did not know how to make use of your high favours, and now I am condemned to live in my incompetence, folded in on myself, as I am now lost; and your hand lies ever more heavily on me. Alas, who will free me from myself? Who will draw me out of this body of death? Who will reach out a hand to me so that I don't get swallowed up by the deep and

---

22. Mt 27:46.

vast ocean? Must I resign myself to being caught up in the storm that pursues me ever more closely?

Must I pronounce my *fiat*, while I gaze at that mysterious person who covers me in sores and does not let up with the hard, bitter, severe and piercing trial, and who gives no time for the old sores to heal, but places new ones on top of the old ones, to the infinite torment of the poor victim? Ah! my Father, for God's sake come to my aid! It rains blood in my inner being, and very often my eye is forced to see it running down my outer being as well. Ah! if only this torture would cease, this condemnation, this humiliation, this confusion! My soul is not steady, and cannot resist and does not know how to resist.

How many things, my Father, would I like to tell you, but the greatness of the pain suffocates me and renders me mute (1089).

147 My Father, my spirit is naked and wretched; my heart is arid and dried-up towards its God; there is hardly any movement in them towards him who out of his goodness created them. I have hardly any faith at all. When the height of the storm rages and the overflowing measure of my wretchedness crushes me, I am powerless to raise myself up on the wings of hope, a virtue so necessary for abandonment to God. I am without charity. Ah! loving God is the consequence of full knowledge, with an active faith. It is also a consequence of the promises into which the soul plunges, finds itself, abandons itself and in which it rests in sweet hope. I have no charity towards my neighbour, because this sort of love is a consequence of love of God, and lacking the latter, all the life-giving sap descends from the branches and every branch dies.

Yes, I am lacking in everything, O Father, without

even the semblance of virtue; I seem to be in a state of fatal lukewarmness, and because of this God justly pushes me further and further from his heart. I see that my ruin is irreparable, because I can see no way out. Alas! I have lost every path, every means, every support, every rule. And if I try to rekindle my burnt-out memory, a mysterious scattering occurs and I become more lost than before, more powerless to raise myself, and the mysterious darkness thickens.

My God, why do you shake and tear this soul, wrapped in clouds and already shaken and confused, with such violence; this soul whose destruction is worked, caused and wished for by your own command and permission? (1036).

148 I declare myself – denying my every wish and knowledge, everything I want and know – I declare myself the most obedient son of my guide in these rigorous ways of the Most High. Is there anything more to say? There certainly is: I ask for strength in my suffering, stripped and bare of all your comfort, that these unconscious but nonetheless greatly desired resolutions might be made more constant and firm and fruitful, at least sufficiently so that your fury is disarmed. Accept them as offerings, my highest Good, to your outraged majesty, but only after you have given them value with your divine virtue. Meanwhile I will strive to find a way of coping with my awful suffering on this bed of sharp and cruel thorns, taking from your hands the food of your rejection and abandonment (1030).

149 I search for God, but where can I find him? Every idea of God as Lord, master, creator, love and life, has faded. He has completely flown, and

I, alas! am lost in the thickest of thick darknesses, going over the scattered remembrances of a lost love again and again, and not able to love anymore. O my Good, where are you? I have lost you, I have become lost by looking for you, because you accepted the open offer I made you, and you have taken everything that was mine, and you hold it in complete mastery. I entrust myself to you and I hope that you will watch over me as I abandon myself completely to the most agonising release of love (1028).

150 My God! My God! The only lament which can express the bitterness of my heart in which I see myself condemned is this: Why have you abandoned me? The modest efforts to hold out, which were made with such ferocious enthusiasm, were in vain. I have no more life, I am not able to bear it any longer or hold out. I must live by you, in you and with you, or I die. Life or death! I am terrified, and I do not know how to push on until who knows when; how long will this terrible time continue? (1051).

151 How can I tell you about the most tormenting sorrow that martyrs my soul? From Thursday I have felt more filled with an extreme anxiety than ever before. I feel that the Lord's hand lies more heavily on me. I feel that the Lord is demonstrating all his powers when he punishes me, and like a leaf carried away by the wind, I am rejected and pursued.

Alas! I cannot go on! I can bear no longer the weight of his justice. I feel myself crushed beneath his powerful hand. Tears are my daily bread. I am agitated, I search for him; but I find him only in the fury of his justice.

O my Father, with complete justification I can say

with the prophet: 'I have come into deep waters, and the storm has submerged me; I have cried and wearied myself in vain; I have become hoarse in vain. Fear and trembling have come over me, and darkness has covered me entirely.'[23] I am stretched out on the bed of my pain, full of woes, seeking my God. But where is he to be found? From my bed of pain and my prison of atonement, I try in vain to come forth into life.

My God, I have lost my way and I have lost you, but where can I find you again? Or have I lost you forever? Have you condemned me to live far from your face for ever? (1027).

152 My Father, help me with your prayers and the prayers of others. How I would prefer not to have to suffer this most bitter sorrow! I have left everything to please God and I would have given my life a thousand times to assure him of my love. And now, O God, how bitter it is to feel in my heart that he is angered with me! I am not able, I cannot find peace in my misfortune. My heart moves irresistibly towards the Lord with all its energy, but an iron hand always pushes me away.

Imagine someone shipwrecked, holding a plank from the ship, whom every surge or gust of wind threatens to drown. Or better, imagine my present state as being like some unhappy person condemned to death, who waits to be taken to the scaffold. My state causes me to suffer even in the depth of night when more than ever I strive to find my God.

I thank God, however, and that no news of my state gets out (1264).

---

23. Cf. Ps 69.

153 I have spent, and spend, hours that are terrible and sorrowful. They think me dead at every turn, both physically and morally. God is unknown to my spirit! O Good of my soul, where are you? Where have you hidden yourself? Where can I find you? Where should I search for you? Do you not see, Jesus, that my soul wants to see you at any price? It seeks you in every place, but you allow yourself to be found only in the fullness of your fury where you fill it with the greatest disturbance and bitterness, leading it to believe how much it belongs to you. Who could express the seriousness of my position? All the things that are clear to me when reflected in your light, I am unable to express in human language. And when I want to stammer something out, the soul thinks it has erred and that it is more than ever distant from the truth of the matter.

My God, are you lost to me forever? I desire to cry out and lament at the top of my voice, but I am very weak and my strength has deserted me. And what will I ever be able to achieve, if I'm not able to make my lament ascend to your throne: 'My God, my God, why have you abandoned me?'[24] (1090).

154 My Father, I am exhausted. I feel that I am being completely crushed under this irresistible force. My God! How much I desire to rest my head on your breast just for one instant, but I am denied this. *Fiat!* My heart is crushed, and torn to pieces by this very great and hard martyrdom.

Ah! Father if you were here, you would not be able to remain so unmoved, like some new Abraham, raising

24. Mt 27:46.

the knife in cold blood to sacrifice his Isaac. You would weep with me and sympathise with me. I waited for your letter like the deer that thirsts, but when I received it, it made my soul bitter (1157).

VI

'OH! WHAT A BEAUTIFUL
THING IT IS TO BECOME A
VICTIM OF LOVE'

(*Letters,* volume I, p. 300)

Suffering and love are the two 'coordinates' of Padre Pio's Spiritual journey. Victim of suffering and victim of love. Both of these formulas occur often, they interlink and complete each other. We could recall, amongst others, the following: 'Love is known in suffering' (p. 328) *; 'I wish only to love and to suffer' (p. 197); 'Oh Jesus, let me love you, let me have all the suffering I desire' (p. 328); 'My soul is melting away through suffering and love, through bitterness and sweetness in equal measure' (p. 1112); 'A mixture of pain and sweetness are wrestling with each other, and reducing my soul into a sweet and bitter swoon' (p. 1113).

The effects of the love of God, which pours itself out into the heart of the creature, which anxiously desires him and searches for him, without ever being able to completely possess him, are described in words and phrases that could be termed 'fiery'; only those used to the language of mystics will be able to understand and appreciate their value, both in themselves and in their literary and Spiritual context. Padre Pio was aware of this: 'My Father, I realise that

---

* As noted before, the page numbers given here refer to the Italian collection of Padre Pio's letters, volume 1.

my words are those of a foolish person; but let them appear as such; it is the love I have for Jesus that has made me so' (p. 499).

It is not possible in this introductory note to present all the ways in which divine love reveals itself, when it has been communicated and freely responded to. The range is enormous: from the delights, sweetness and joys of divine consolations so rich and so numerous that they caused Padre Pio to describe them as an 'indigestion', which are the fruit of the soul's intimate conversations with God, through to the highest expressions of the mystical life, like swooning, the joining of hearts, the wound of love, the trans-verberation (this mystical event is described in number 195), substantial touches (see number 196), stigmata…

The life of Padre Pio was without doubt a life of love in which the notion of victim found its full expression and realisation. The passages in this chapter are an authentic and authoritative illustration of the following self-portrait by Padre Pio: 'The one thought of my soul, which torments it without ceasing, is to love God… It wants to love God in spite of everything' (p. 758); 'Jesus is so infatuated with my heart, that he makes me burn with his divine fire, with his fire of love' (p. 316).

❧

155 I feel continually that my frozen body encloses a burning heart (285).

156 All the supernatural things that I have received always produced in me a notable

benefit. Such heavenly favours have produced in me, besides the effects belonging to each individual favour, three principal effects:

– a wonderful knowledge of God and his incomparable greatness;

– a great knowledge of myself, and a profound sense of humility when I realise how bold I was in offending such a holy Father;

– and a great contempt for all the things of the earth and a great love for God and virtue (423).

157 What I mean, in utmost truth and clarity, is that my heart loves very much more than the intellect knows. I am certain of this, and no doubt about it has ever surfaced in my mind. I do not think I lie if I assert that I have never been tempted about it. I am very sure that my will loves this most tender Spouse; after the sacred Scriptures, there is nothing else about which I am so certain (418).

158 If I consider the love of Jesus, on one hand, and my ingratitude, on the other, I wish to say, my Father, that if my love cannot equal his, may he love me nevertheless: only in this way does my guilt seem to be covered over. But if Jesus does not love me, what will become of me? If I do not love Jesus and he loves me no more? This is a terrifying prospect, and so I plead always with Jesus that he continue to love me and think of me, even if I am not able to love him as he deserves (236).

159 But long live Jesus! Who even in the thick of these dark thoughts, which ought to cast me into desperation, gives my soul such a peace that I have rarely felt as I do at the present. Yes, my Father,

Jesus is sweetness which wishes to fill my entire heart. But, how is this! Does he not see my ingratitude? Does he not see my heart, which is without devotion? He not only sustains me, but he loves me with a singular love.

And how should I not love him? Let my heart speak for me... my Father, help me! I feel that if Jesus continues to burn my heart and innards before he unites me to himself, I will not be able to resist and I will go on my way... (289).

160 Jesus almost always asks love of me. And my heart more than my mouth replies to him: 'Oh my Jesus, I wish...', and I am unable to continue. But in the end I exclaim: 'Yes Jesus, I love you. In this moment I feel I love you and at the same time feel the need to love you more; but Jesus, I have no more love in my heart, you know that I have given everything to you. If you want more love, take this heart of mine and fill it with your love, and then command me to love you, I will not refuse; in fact, I beg you to do so, I desire it' (266).

161 I feel, my Father, that love will eventually conquer me. My soul runs the risk of separating itself from the body, because it is unable to love Jesus sufficiently on the earth. So wounded is the soul with love for Jesus. So am I made ill by love. I experience continually the bitter pain of that ardour that burns and does not consume. Tell me, if you can, the remedy for my present state of soul (297).

162 Many other times I have felt myself smothered by a very violent onslaught, I felt myself pining for God, I thought I was just about

to die. All of this comes not from some consideration or thought, but from an internal flame, and from a love that is so excessive, that if God did not come quickly to help me I would be consumed by it (422).

163 Many times it happens that when the continual thought of God, which is always with me, leaves my mind for a little, I feel something from our Lord touching the core of my soul. This happens in such a piercing, yet gentle manner, that more often than not I am compelled to weep tears of sorrow because of my infidelity, mingled with tears of tenderness because I have such a good Father who is so attentive in recalling me to his presence (420).

164 Talk to me at length, O my Father, about everything and if you find me at fault, do not remain silent. Raise your voice high, punish me again: I want to love Jesus as I should. I desire this love. I know that I love him, but, O Lord, how inferior is my actual love to the desire that I have! In reality, shouldn't the former be greater than the latter? (558).

165 Father, may I at least be allowed to unburden myself to you. I am crucified by love! I can take no more! This is a very dainty food for those who are used to coarse fare. And it is exactly this that continually produces such strong Spiritual indigestion, to such a point that it makes the poor soul groan with an acutely felt mixture of suffering and love. This poor wretch is not able to adjust himself to the new way in which the Lord deals with it. And so the kiss and the touch, which I would say are now very full and which this most loving heavenly Father imprints on the soul, become a cause of great sorrow (545).

166 How unhappy, my Father, is the state of a soul which God has made infirm by his love! For charity's sake, pray to the Lord to set an end to my days, I no longer feel strong enough to go on like this. I can see no other remedy to my heart's illness than to be consumed by these flames that burn and never consume (526).

167 O God, sovereign of my heart, only centre of my every happiness! How much longer must I wait to see the unveiling of your ineffable beauty? You have pierced my soul with the thunderbolt of your love; you are that cruel one who opens profound wounds in my heart that cannot be seen; you kill me and do not bother to raise me up in your homeland! What comfort do you give this soul, which cannot find you here below and which can never have peace, distant from you? (656).

168 When, O my dear Father, will Jesus consume me completely in his holy love? When will I be completely consumed by the divine flames? When can I unite myself intimately to him so that I can break out into an entirely new song, the song of victory? When will this civil strife between Satan and the poor soul finish, the soul that wants to belong entirely to its heavenly spouse? (923).

169 I understand very well that the soul can only enter into its eternal rest when, lost forever in that immense ocean of goodness, it will know that he knows, love what he loves and enjoy only those things which make God himself blessed (650).

170 Bear with your exile, because it is an exile that God wishes. What a great gain this is for you. I will live in this cruel life, O my Jesus, in silence and hope will be my strength, as long as this wretched life endures. While you, O my creator and my God, make the beautiful flame of your love burn in my heart... O only centre of my every happiness, O my God! How much longer must I wait?... You see, O Lord, that my illness is without remedy... When then, O Lord, When? How much longer? (650).

171 O holy souls, free from every anxiety and already enjoying that torrent of sovereign sweetness in heaven, O how much I envy your happiness! Alas, for pity's sake, since you are so close to the fountain of life, since you see me dying of thirst in this world here below, favour me with a little of that freshest of waters.

Ah! O holy souls, I confess have I spent my portion very badly, very badly have I guarded the gem of great price. But long live God! I feel that for this fault there is also a remedy. Well, blessed souls, give me some help. Because I am not able to find what my soul needs during rest in the night, I, too, will rise like the spouse in the holy Canticle and seek him who my soul loves: 'I will rise now and go about the city; I will seek the Beloved of my soul.'[25] I will always seek him, I will seek him in everything and I will not stop in any, until I find him on the threshold of his Kingdom... (676).

172 Who would ever be able to control or put out this fire, whose flames burn so ardently for you in my breast? Ah! O Lord, why do you hide!

---

25. Cf. Song 3:2.

You understand what confusion and agitation takes possession of all the soul's powers and feelings! You see that my poor soul cannot bear the cruel torture of this abandonment, because you have made it fall in love with you too deeply, infinite beauty! (675).

173 I accept all the torments of this earth, O my God, and I desire my portion. But I will never resign myself to be separated from you on account of a lack of love. Ah! for pity's sake, do not allow this poor soul to err; do not allow my hope to fail. Do not let me be ever separated from you, and if I am now distant from you without knowing it, bring me back this instant; strengthen my intellect, O my God, so that I might know myself thoroughly and know the great love that you have shown me, and so that I might be able to enjoy eternally the sovereign beauty of your divine face (675).

174 In certain moments such is the fire that devours me inside, that I strive as hard as I can to distance myself from them [Jesus and Mary], so that I can go in search of water and ice to cool me inside. But alas! my Father, I immediately realise that I have become very unhappy, because I then feel more than ever that I am not free. The chains that my eyes do not see, I feel holding me very closely to Jesus and his beloved Mother. And in these moments I am seized more often than not by a fit of anger; I feel blood flowing to the heart and thence to the head; I am tempted to shout in their faces and call the Son cruel, and the Mother a tyrant! (357).

175 In these days, which are so solemn for me on account of the Feast of the Heavenly

Child, I have often been taken by those excesses of divine love, that make my poor heart grow so very weak. I understand all Jesus' kindness towards me, and so I have addressed my usual prayer to him with greater confidence: 'O Jesus, I wish to love you, I wish to suffer in reality as much as I desire to; I wish to make you happy and to make up in some way for the ingratitude people show towards you!'

But in my heart I hear Jesus' voice very clearly: 'My son, love is known in suffering; you will feel it deeply in the spirit, and you will feel it even more deeply in the body.' These words, my Father, remain obscure to me (328).

176 There comes upon me, also, a great desire to serve God with perfection. This, too, happens without any sort of consideration or thought on my part, and in an instant. The soul does not understand where the courage that it feels comes from. Such desires consume the soul interiorly, through a clear light that God gives it, because it cannot render God the service that he desires. Then all finishes in the delights that God himself sends to flood the soul (422).

177 *Bluebeard* does not want to leave me alone at any cost, rather he always finds new ways of making it hard for me. But it is true that Jesus is also with me. If you will allow me the expression I am about to use, I seem continually to have 'indigestion caused by consolations' (250).

178 I have continual indigestion caused by divine consolations. At times, I feel that I am dying of them because of too much sweetness, and

I am on the point of telling Jesus with St Augustine: '*Eia, Domine, moriar ut te videam*'[26] (264).

179 By the will of God I continue to experience bad health. But what torments me most are the strong, sharp pains in my chest. At times they give so much bother that it seems to me they want to shatter my spine and chest.

Yet Jesus does not forget to sweeten my sufferings in another way, that is by speaking to my heart. O yes, my Father, how good Jesus is to me! O what precious moments these are ! It is a happiness so great, I do not know what to compare it with, a happiness that the Lord gives me to taste almost only in moments of affliction (107).

180 In these moments [when Jesus speaks to my heart], more than ever, everything in the world wearies me and is a burden; I desire nothing but to love and suffer. Yes, my Father, even in the midst of so much suffering I am happy, because it seems to me that I can feel my heart beat with Jesus' heart. Now you can imagine just how much consolation the heart receives from the almost certain knowledge that it possesses Jesus (197).

181 When I ask Jesus what I have done to merit so many consolations, he smiles at me and repeats that nothing is denied such an intercessor. He asks only love as a recompense. But don't I owe this to him for gratitude? Oh, if only I could please him a little, my Father, in the same way that he makes me happy! He is so infatuated with my heart, that he makes

---

26. 'Lord, let me die that I might see you.' Cf. Augustine, *Confessions*, I,5,5.

me burn completely with his divine fire, with his fire of love. What is this fire that so completely lays siege to me? My Father, if Jesus makes us so happy on earth, what will it be like in heaven? (316).

182 My heart wants to love, it strives to do so; but it cannot find a way. Poor thing. Perhaps it finds itself outside its centre, and this is the reason why it does not know where to put itself (839).

183 I desire nothing more than to die or to love God: death or love, since life without this love is worse than death; for me it would then be more unbearable than it is at the moment (841).

184 I must, however, confess that I am happy even in the midst of these afflictions, because the sweetness that our good Jesus gives me to taste nearly every day is so very great (200).

185 My Father, with tormented soul I submit to living, only in order not to sicken Jesus or to go against the orders of my Superior. But why is it not given to me to love him with sincerity and serenity of spirit? I feel alone, and a huge emptiness that frightens me is continually present in my soul. This poor heart is unquiet and does not know where to put itself.

I place it with Jesus, and it is still not satisfied. What misfortune is this? Oh, if only I could love Jesus, how happy I would be! But this comfort is taken from me, too, and I cannot find the way to get to him! (841).

186 I am submerged in an ocean of fire. My reopened wound bleeds and bleeds. This alone would be enough to kill me more than a thousand times over. O my God, why do I not die? Or do you not see that for the soul that you afflict, life itself is a torment? You are cruel, too, you who remain deaf to the cries of those who suffer and do not comfort them! But what am I saying?... Pardon me, Father, I am not myself; I do not know what I am saying. The excess of suffering that causes my ever-open wound, enrages me against my will, it makes me no longer myself and drives me delirious. And I am powerless to resist (1072).

187 First of all, I must confess that for me it is a great disgrace not to know how to describe this volcano, which is constantly burning and which burns me. Jesus put it in this tiny heart of mine, and I can neither describe it nor quench it. The explanation is simple: I am devoured by the love of God and the love of neighbour. God is always fixed in my mind and imprinted on my heart. I never lose sight of him; I admire his beauty, his smiles and the troubles he gives, his mercy, his vengeance, or better, the rigours of his justice (1247).

188 I know very well that I never had anything that could have drawn our most sweet Jesus' attention. His goodness alone has filled my soul with so many good things. He hardly ever leaves me. He follows me everywhere. He revives my life, which had been poisoned by sin. He clears from me the dense clouds which had covered my soul on account of sin.

During the night, on closing my eyes, I see the veil which covers paradise lower itself down. And made joyful by this vision I sleep with a smile of sweet beatitude on my lips, in a perfect calm, waiting for my little companion to come and wake me so that we can sing together the morning praises to the Delight of our hearts.

Oh! my Father, if what you know of my state awakens in you any thought other than that of compassion, take it, I beg you, to my Beloved on my behalf as a mark of recognition and gratitude (307).

189 The heavenly persons have not ceased to visit me and to give me a foretaste of the rapture of the blessed. And if the mission of our guardian angels is great, mine is without doubt greater since I must try to explain other tongues competently (304).

190 I have spent all of last night with the loving Jesus. I suffer much, as well, but in a way which is very different from the suffering I experienced during the preceding night. This state of suffering is one that is not painful at all; my trust in God grows ever greater. I feel ever more drawn to Jesus. Without any fire nearby, I felt that I was burning interiorly. Without anything holding me, I felt myself close to Jesus and bound to him. I felt myself burnt by a thousand flames that made me live and made me die. Thus I suffered, living and dying continuously (293).

191 The Child Jesus came, and I said that I wanted only to do his will. He consoled me and encouraged me regarding the sufferings of the previous night. O God, how my heart beat, how my cheeks burnt, in the presence of this heavenly Child! (292).

192 Let me tell you what happened on Friday (23.8.1912). I had stayed in Church to make my thanksgiving for the Mass, when all of a sudden I felt my heart wounded by a dart of fire so living and burning that I thought I would die of it.

I cannot find the right words to help you understand the intensity of this flame; I am completely powerless to express myself. Would you believe it? The soul, victim of these consolations, has become mute. It seemed to me that an invisible strength immersed me completely in fire... my God, what fire! what sweetness!

I have felt many of these transports of love, and I have remained as if out of this world at different times. At other times this fire has been less intense. But if this time I had remained in this state for a second, an instant more, my soul would have been separated from my body... it would have departed with Jesus.

Oh, what a beautiful thing it is to become a victim of love. But how fares my soul at the moment? '*Mon cher père, à présent Jésus a retiré son javelot de feu, mais la blessure est mortelle...*'[27]

193 I was with difficulty able to go to the divine Prisoner to celebrate. Mass being finished, I was with Jesus during my thanksgiving. Oh, how sweet was the conversation held in paradise this morning! It was such that, although I wished to try and tell him everything, I was not able; there were such things that cannot be translated into human

---

27. 'My dear Father, at present Jesus has withdrawn his lance of fire, but the wound is mortal...'

language without losing their profound and heavenly meaning. The heart of Jesus and my heart, if you will allow me the expression, fused together. No longer two hearts were beating, but one alone. My heart disappeared, like a drop of water in the sea. Jesus was its paradise, its king. The joy in me was so intense, so profound, that I could contain it no longer; the most delightful tears streamed from my eyes.

Yes, my Father, humankind cannot understand that when paradise is poured into the heart – this afflicted, excited, weak and mortal heart – it cannot bear it without weeping. Yes, I repeat it, it was the joy alone that filled my heart and caused me to weep for such a long time.

Believe me, this visit completely consoled me. Long live the divine Prisoner! (273).

194 I am alone by day, I am alone by night and no ray of light comes to illumine me. No drop of relief ever comes to refresh the flame that devours me continually without ever consuming me completely.

Once only have I felt in the most secret and intimate part of my spirit a thing so delicate, that I do not know how I could get you to believe it. At first, my soul felt his presence, without being able to see. Then, I would say, he came so close to the soul that it fully perceived his touch. This is just as it happens, to give a comparison, when our body touches another body. I don't know what else to say, only to confess to you that I was at first seized by the greatest fright, that slowly became a heavenly rapture. I seemed no longer to be in the pilgrim state, and I couldn't say if I noticed whether I was still in this body or not when it happened. Only God knows, and I don't know how better to get you to believe that this really happened (757).

195 In accordance with this [obedience], I have decided to tell you what happened to me from the evening of the fifth and all during the sixth of this current month [August 1918].

Exactly what happened in this period of the greatest martyrdom, I am not really able to tell you. I was confessing our lads at five in the evening, when suddenly I was filled with fear at the appearance of a heavenly personage who presented himself before the eyes of the intellect. He held in his hand a kind of tool, similar to an extremely long blade of iron with a well-sharpened point from which fire seemed to be coming out. Seeing all this, and observing the said person hurl this implement with great violence into my soul, was an extraordinary experience. With difficulty I emitted a groan; I felt I was dying. I asked the lad to go because I was feeling bad and didn't have the strength to continue.

This torment lasted without interruption until the morning of the seventh. What I suffered in this sorrowful period I cannot say. I saw that even my innards were hurt and stretched by that instrument; and everything was put to iron and fire.

From that day on I have been mortally wounded. I feel a wound deep in my soul which is always open and racks me thoroughly with pain (1065).

196 I can find no escape from my present state, which continues without any pause. During the Feast [of *Corpus Domini*, 30.5.1918], I found myself placed in a state which is excruciating beyond words. And this is what happened.

I remember that on the morning of the said day at the Offertory of the holy Mass I received a breath of life. I couldn't even begin to explain what happened inside me in that fleeting moment: I felt myself shake all over, I was filled with a great terror and I very nearly lost my life. Then I was overcome by a complete calm such as I have never experienced before.

All this terror, shaking and calm, succeeding each other, was not caused by anything seen, but by something that I felt touch me in the most intimate and secret part of my soul.

I cannot tell you anything else about this event. May it please God to help you understand this event as it happened in its reality (1053).

197 My Father, I feel myself drowning in the immense, open sea of my Beloved's love. I suffer from continual indigestion. And the bitterness of this love is sweet, and its burden, light. But this does not mean that my soul in feeling this great transport of love has the wherewithal to carry the burden, and I feel crushed and conquered.

My small heart feels unable to contain this immense love within itself. It is true that God is inside and outside. But, my God, when he pours himself into the small vessel of my existence, I suffer torments because I am unable to contain all of him. The internal walls of my heart feel close to bursting, and I wonder that this hasn't happened already.

And when this love finds itself unable to enter inside my small vessel in its entirety, it pours itself all down the sides. How can one bear being completely covered by the infinite?

I feel that I am dying, my God! and you see this frail existence being extinguished, this existence that consumed itself for you; and, meanwhile, you remain indifferent. Am I not right therefore to call you tyrannical, cruel? Alas, what am I saying?... Pardon me, O God, my love! I am beside myself and I do not know what I am saying.

You have made me impatient, you have conquered me, you have burnt all my insides, you have introduced a river of fire inside me. How can I not complain, if you yourself provoke me and put my fragility to the test? My Father, do not be horrified by these impious blasphemies, because I cannot contain myself. But the Beloved himself will not remove his gaze from his creature on account of this (1122).

198 My Father, I cannot survive this suffering: when it gets worse I feel myself annihilated, I feel my life ebbing away, and in these moments I couldn't tell you whether I am alive or not. I am outside myself. Pain and sweetness are mingled together, reducing the soul to a sweet-and-bitter swoon.

The Beloved's embraces, which are still coming one after another in great profusion – and almost without respite and without measure and without sparing me – are unable to extinguish the soul's great torment at feeling itself incapable of bearing the weight of infinite love. And it is precisely in these periods – which are almost without interruption – that the soul utters things to this divine Lover which I am horrified to pronounce when I have returned to myself (1113).

199 I find it almost impossible to explain how my Beloved works. The immense strength of infinite love has finally conquered the hardness of my soul, and I am annihilated and reduced to powerlessness.

He pours all of himself into the tiny vessel of this creature, who suffers an unspeakable torment and feels itself unable to bear the weight of this immense love. Alas! who will come and lift me up? How can I carry the infinite in my tiny heart? How can I keep him restricted in the narrow cell of my soul?

My soul is being torn to pieces by suffering and love, by bitterness and sweetness at the same time. How can I bear this immense work of the Most High?

I possess him in me; and this causes me to exult and irresistibly leads me to say with the most holy Virgin: 'My spirit exults in God my saviour'.[28]

I possess him in me, and I feel everything, and I feel the strength to say with the Spouse of the sacred Canticle: 'I found him whom my soul loves; I held him and would not let him go.'[29]

But when I see myself incapable of bearing the weight of this infinite love, of squeezing all of it into my small existence, I am filled with a terror that I will have to leave him because I am not able to contain it in the narrow little house of my heart.

This thought (which I must say has not been infused by God – I have myself taken the measure of my strength and know it to be very limited, incapable of keeping the divine Lover close to me and powerless to keep hold of him) tortures me, distresses me and makes my heart beat so violently against my chest, it almost shatters it (1112f).

28. Lk 1:47.
29. Song 3:4.

200 I am besieged on all sides, forced by a thousand difficulties to search, in weariness and despair, the very one who wounds me cruelly and continues to afflict me without ever letting himself be seen. Contradicted in every way, closed in on all sides, tempted in every manner, totally deprived of another's help, evil or good, I do not know: I struggle impotently in my search for the Highest Good, but what am I saying?... every search is in vain.

Ah! my Father, that volcano that I feel keeps renewing itself ever more in my spirit. I still feel it burn all my insides. In short, everything is being put to iron and to fire: both spirit and body. I, who have a soul full of sorrow and eyes dried up and withered from weeping, am forced to be present, against my will, at this torture, at this complete decay. I am unable to turn my eyes away because I am powerless to react in any way. Alas, unhappy one! Who will free me from this body of death? Who will pull me from this blazing furnace that burns with an inextinguishable flame and never consumes? (1096).

201 Do you imagine that there could be a little consolation for this soul? It is entirely rejected from the face of the Lord, and it finds everything to be just. It sees clearly that its loss is irreparable; it does not know how to reconcile itself to such a great loss; it wants to love the God who pushes it away; even more, it strives to love him, and its one thought, that torments it without a moment's respite, is to love the God it has so greatly offended. In spite of everything it wants to love him, even though it sees its loss as irreparable (758).

VII

'… AND YOUR NEIGHBOUR
AS YOURSELF'

(Mt 22:39)

Padre Pio bore witness vigorously and effectively to the second dimension of the divine commandment on love (cf. Mt 22:36-40). Christian life has an authentic 'horizontal dimension' – which is not divorced from the essential 'vertical dimension' that gives this life its value and reason for existing at all. This 'horizontal dimension' has two different but connected aspects: the first aims at saving and sanctifying one's neighbour's soul; the second aims at being compassionate and relieving the distress and sufferings of their body.

In both these aspects, the love of Padre Pio went out to his neighbour, and to those who provide stimulus and guidance for all Christians, but principally to priests in the exercise of their apostolic ministry.

God and the human person are the two poles of attraction in the human heart which at times even seem to clash, but only apparently, creating situations of dramatic intensity. Such situations 'lacerate the soul', which desires to immerse itself in the ocean of divine love, but at the same time 'is transported dizzily to live for its neighbours'.

Padre Pio was very satisfied and 'extremely joyful' on account of the Spiritual fruits of his priestly ministry, and his soul felt attracted by a 'very great compassion' towards the poor and by a 'very vehement desire' to help them in their material needs and their afflictions of the spirit.

202 What about the brothers, then? Alas! how many times, not to say every single time, it has been my task to say to God the Judge as Moses did: 'Either pardon this people or remove me from the book of life.'[30] What a terrible thing it is to live from the heart! One must die in every moment a death that kills us only in the sense that dying we live and living we die. Alas! Who will free me from this devouring fire? Pray, my Father, so that a torrent of water might come to relieve me a little from this devouring flame that burns in my heart without respite (1248).

203 My Father, if I were able to fly, I would like to raise my voice, I would like to cry out to all with all the strength my voice can command: 'Love Jesus, who deserves to be loved' (293).

204 Alas, my Father, how many offences does Jesus receive from human beings! I feel my blood run cold when I consider how badly we respond to Jesus' love. One could say that it is as if Jesus never loved, considering all the hatred that people bear him. How many times have I raised my voice to our heavenly Father and asked that, for the sake of Jesus' gentleness or the reverence due to his person, he either put an end to the world or bring these iniquities to a close.

---

30. The words here attributed to Moses do not occur in the Scriptures in this exact form; cf. Num. 11:12ff.

He is omnipotent, and he can do it. Plead with him yourself for this end (414).

205 I feel inflamed by such a lively and ardent desire to please God, and filled with such a strong fear of falling into some small imperfection, that I would like to fly from all interaction with the creatures. At the same time another desire rises in my heart, like a giant: the desire to stand among all the peoples and to proclaim with a loud voice who this great God of mercy is (368).

206 For the soul inflamed with divine charity, taking care of one's neighbours' needs is a fever that consumes it slowly. It would give its life a thousand times, if this meant that even one more soul might give more praise to the Lord.

I, too, feel this fever devouring me. But, alas! my God, how different is my own motive which urges me to do this. I, too, like this soul sigh to give my life to help my neighbour and to glorify God. Not, however, for the same reason, since I am so far from being anything like these souls. What urges me to call upon death with every vow I know where my neighbour or the glory of God are concerned, is that, having lived so badly, I fear to live any more and I am very wearied by the tribulations of this exile (414).

207 I cannot deny anyone. How could I do this if the Lord himself wants it and if he denies me nothing that I ask of him? (906).

208 Believe me, Father, the violent outbursts that at times I have given in to are caused by this hard prison sentence, let us call it also a 'fortunate

sentence'. How is it possible to see God grieving over evil and not to grieve equally oneself? When one sees God on the point of launching his thunderbolts, what other way is there to ward them off than to raise a hand to hold back his arm, and to extend an impassioned hand to one's neighbour? This is done with a twofold motive: that they might desist from doing evil and that they move themselves – and quickly – because the hand of the Judge is about to bring itself down on them.

You must believe as well, however, that in this moment I am not all shaken on the inside, nor do I feel diminished or changed. The only thing I feel is to have and to want what God wants. In him I always feel at rest, at least interiorly; exteriorly I sometimes feel a little uncomfortable (1247).

209 You tell me that I have threatened to think only of myself. I don't know if and when I might have said it and to whom it was said, but I can tell you that it wasn't said in the sense that you have taken it. My actions prove it. I have worked, I want to work; I have prayed, I want to pray; I have kept watch, I want to keep watch; I have wept and want always to weep for my brothers in exile. I know this is not much, I understand that; but this is what I know how to do. This is what I am able to do, and it is all that I can do (1243).

210 Midnight strikes and, exhausted by the many, many labours that fill the entire day, I take my pen in hand to tell you something about my soul. I do this in order not to fail your desire, that is to me a command.

Poor me! I can find no rest. Tired and immersed in

the greatest bitterness, in the most desperate desolation, the most anxious distress – I am not, of course unable to find my God again, no! but unable to gain all my brothers for God. What must I do? I do not know. I suffer, I seek their salvation from God, but I do not know if God accepts any of my groans. In fact, I would add that sometimes I doubt whether I myself am in God's grace. This most painful doubt is strengthened by an obscure fear as to whether God rewards all my strivings to take care of others' miseries. It is also strengthened by my observation that my heart is always arid, restless, gasping when it sees so many souls suffering and is unable to raise them up (1152).

211 Beg Father Provincial to send many labourers into the vineyard of the Lord, because it is truly cruel and tyrannical to send away hundreds and even thousands of souls every day. These souls come from far away with the sole aim of being cleansed of their sins, but cannot attain their desire because of the lack of priest confessors (1147).

212 I do not have a free minute. All my time is spent releasing my brothers from Satan's snares. Blessed be God.

I beg you, therefore, not to afflict me with calls to charity, because the greatest charity consists in snatching souls conquered by Satan to gain them for Christ. And this is precisely what I do assiduously day and night (1145).

213 You will understand how extremely busy we have been with confessions and instructions as the older children prepare themselves to draw near

to the sacrament of Confirmation. Seeing some hundreds of people approaching the sacraments is a deeply moving thing, enough to provoke tears. I am extremely joyful because of the good that so many souls have received from the Father of Lights. Let God be praised eternally for it (471).

214 Rejoice with me in the sweet Lord because of the most abundant harvest of souls in these days of sweet propitiation! I am truly most satisfied and full of joy because of it. May God be blessed for it! (1197).

215 If only I could, as I once did, find a little relief in my one, ardent desire to leave this exile to be united with Jesus! Today, this is given to me no more. I find myself transported rather headily to live for my brothers, and as a consequence to intoxicate and fill myself with these sufferings that I nevertheless continue irresistibly to mourn for (1196).

216 My Father, what sorrowful and woeful days I see ahead! How awful Christmas will be for me this year! I am prepared for everything, as long as Jesus is happy and he saves the souls of my brothers, especially those he has entrusted to me (1189).

217 I can tell you nothing more about my spirit at present, other than Jesus has begun to let me feel how sweet it is to live and think for one's brothers (1184).

218 The two forces that seem to be opposed – that of wanting to be useful to one's brothers in exile, and that of wanting to die so as to be united

to Christ – I have lately felt grow to enormous dimensions in the highest point of the spirit. They lacerate my soul and rob it of any peace. This peace is not the innermost, but even if the peace they touch – so to speak – is only on the outside, I recognise how necessary this peace is for me if I am to able to go about my business with greater sweetness and anointing (1181).

219 I am placed in the greatest desolation. All alone, I bear the burdens of all; I feel that I am unable to bring relief of spirit to those whom Jesus has sent me: the thought that I can see so many souls who wish recklessly to excuse their wickedness against the will of the highest Good distresses me; it tortures me, it torments me, it wears my brain out and tears my heart to pieces. O God! I feel that such a thorn has been driven into my heart! (1181).

220 Ah! again you have had occasion to understand how cruel a torment this soul suffers on seeing the great offences that humankind gives in these sad times, and the horrendous ingratitude with which your tokens of love are repaid, and the little or no thought that the truly blind give to themselves on losing you.

My God, my God! We should also say that these no longer trust you, since they so rudely deny you the debt of their love. Alas! my God, when will the moment come when this soul can see your kingdom of love re-established?… When will you bring my torment to an end? (676).

221 The state of my soul, thanks be to God, with its ups and down, progresses as normal.

One thing alone seems to me particularly unusual: great Spiritual pleasure is followed by great Spiritual desolation; this change is normally caused by humankind's poor response to the favours of heaven. I would like, I would really like to do something more for them, to render them acceptable to the heart of God. But I feel powerless, as if my wings were clipped. I suffer because of this, it is true, but I would suffer even more if the Lord were to remove me from this difficult trial (1174).

222 I always work diligently, and with more responsibility [than the others]. It is already one in the morning as I trace these few lines. I have already been working for nineteen hours without a break. Patience! (1158).

223 I am tired, extremely tired, of crying out to God to make himself clear at long last, to get him to yield to my supplications, to my cries. Ah! I do understand that one who is not worthy of his love does not deserve to be heard; but couldn't he listen to the pleading of one who pleads without any self-interest, and who pleads only for the benefit of his neighbour. I hope that a child's heart might be more tender and pliant towards its poverty-stricken brothers. For this reason, I will importune the heavenly child, and I expect much from him (1154).

224 Your letter, so full of affection, brought me some relief in a moment of intense struggle. Relief because, if I have felt the burden of the sacred ministry weigh heavily, and I have felt keenly the responsibility and fear of not following God's will in carrying out the ministry assigned to me by his divine

mercy, I am comforted by the thought that my Father is always concerned about the well-being of my soul. I hope that Jesus will not only illuminate me as I guide the souls that he has entrusted me and sustain me and comfort me in adversity, but he himself will make up for my deficiencies. Continue to importune the divine Heart, so that it sustain me and prevent my collapsing under the burden of work and bitterness (1227).

225 Commend me to the divine mercy, so that the labour which presses on me and oppresses me continually without interruption, by night and by day, and my physical ills, which have been getting worse for some time, do not make me collapse. My work always concerns suffering and I have so much work that I have no time to look to myself, and it is truly a miracle that I don't lose my head over it all (1215).

226 The storms that I described to you in my other letters become ever more furious and it seems that I might be swept away at any moment. The only support that remains to me in the midst of the howling of the storm is authority alone, unadorned and bare, without comfort and without nourishment for the spirit. I receive a little indirect comfort only when I admire the abundant harvest in the house of the Lord. On the other hand, I feel the strength to renounce everything, as long as souls return to Jesus and love Jesus (1210).

227 O God! O God! where are my thoughts flying to? What will happen to those unhappy children of yours, still my brothers, who may already have merited your thunderbolts? You know, O

my sweet Redeemer how many times the remembrance of your divine face, angered by these unhappy brothers of mine, has made my blood run cold with fright – more than the thought of the eternal punishment and all the sorrows of hell.

I have always begged you, trembling, as I am pleading with you at present, to withdraw your thunderous gaze from my unhappy brothers for the sake of your mercy... You yourself have said, O my sweet Lord, that 'Love is as strong as death, and as relentless as the grave',[31] and so look on these dead brothers with eyes of ineffable sweetness, bind them to you with a firm clasp of love.

May all these who are truly dead rise again, O Lord. O Jesus, Lazarus did not ask you to raise him: the prayers of a sinful woman were enough. Oh! here is another example, O my divine Lord – a sinful woman and guilty beyond comparison – of one who pleads for the many dead who do not bother to pray to you themselves to be resurrected.

You know, O my Lord and my King, the severe torture that these other Lazaruses cause me: call them with a voice so powerful that life is given to them and that at your command they come out of the tomb of their foul pleasures.

Do it, O Lord, and so all will bless the riches of your mercy...

My Father, once again it has dawned on me that I was not just talking, but writing. Ah! for charity's sake, forgive and sympathise with one whose heart is aching. And you must pity me all the more because the illness from which I suffer is of itself incurable.

---

31. Song 8:6.

You exhort me to offer myself as a victim to the Lord for poor sinners. I have already made this offer and I continually renew it, every day. But how is it that the Lord does not answer me? I have even offered my life in return for their salvation, and yet the Lord allows me to continue to live. Therefore does this mean that the holocaust I offered him – and even now I offer my whole self to him – has not pleased him? (677).

228 I cannot hide from you the constriction my heart feels in seeing so many souls apostatising from Jesus. And what makes my heart's blood run even colder is that the only reason many of these souls become distant from God, source of living water, is because they are starved of the divine Word. The harvest is plentiful but the workers are few. Who will gather in the harvest, which is almost ready, from the field of the Church? Will it be scattered all over the ground because of the shortage of workers? Will it be gathered in by the emissaries of Satan, who are unfortunately very plentiful and very active? Ah! the most sweet God will never allow this to happen; he will take pity on human misery, which is becoming very great (466).

229 Moreover, be calm and never refuse in any way, or for any motive, to give alms to anyone who happens to be there; and not only this, but when the right opportunities present themselves, offer your very self. The Lord desires as much, and you should strive to do it (1213).

230 It seems to me that God has poured in the depths of this soul many graces regarding the poor and needy. The great compassion that my soul feels when I see someone in need, gives birth in its very centre to a most vehement desire to help them; and if I were to heed the promptings of my will I would strip myself down to rags to clothe them.

If I know that someone is afflicted, whether in soul or body, what would I not do for the Lord to see them free of their ills? To see them saved I would take upon myself all their afflictions, giving them in return the fruits of such sufferings, if the Lord would allow it (462).

231 I exhort you not to sadden yourself at all because of my distress if you don't want to add more sadness to that which I already feel (502).

232 The sweet Jesus will not leave her in this state without consoling her. May the God of goodness be praised and blessed! Knowing how bitter these griefs are, and how much greater the crown gained through them, I am tempted to ask Jesus to send me the sorrows that are prepared for her; but I realise that I am being too selfish, longing to have the better part for myself. But let us ask Jesus, that if this would give him a little glory, then he should do it (380).

233 I am distressed only in seeing you so greatly tried. I feel all your afflictions as if they were mine. Knowing of all your troubles, I spontaneously ask the Lord either to command your misfortune to relent a little, or to increase your strength to resist, with sweet resignation to his most holy will. I beg him more and more to let these trials, which are reserved for you, fall on my head, while the crown and prize earned by such trials be reserved for you. But while I am praying

in this way and sorrowing, I also feel a Spiritual joy because of the great love that God bears you. And the storm that roars about your head and causes such confusion is a certain sign of this love (1010).

234 Courage, then, and forward! Jesus wants to make a tiny, little hole in your spirit through this trial, therefore be grateful to him for it. Before, however, this letter arrives at its destination – as I have unlimited trust in our heavenly Father – this struggle will at least in part become much less fierce, and it will therefore be easier to bear it, as the sweet Jesus has, in accordance with my willing offer, made me a participant in it (485).

235 I am very, very sad to hear that you are in poor health and I am praying to the Lord for your recovery. Not being able to do anything else for you, I have frequently offered myself to the Lord for you, as a victim. And now that I know that you are ill, with greater fervour I frequently renew my offer to Jesus (707).

236 I cannot hide from you how I feel all your anxieties as my own and how, almost by a blind instinct, I am impelled to beg the divine mercy to command this torment to stop (484).

237 I was very sorry to hear that you are in a bad way physically, and I beg Jesus incessantly to send this trial to me, quadrupling it if he wills, and to give you all the merit. If this is for the best, I would be delighted to take on the role of Simon of Cyrene for you. I beg you, too, to implore Jesus to grant this petition (1259).

VIII

'OUR BEAUTIFUL VIRGIN MARY'

(*Letters*, volume 1, p. 182)

Devotion to Mary Most Holy is without doubt one of the essential components of Padre Pio's spirituality. The passages selected from his letters which appear in this chapter are proof of this.

With a child's tenderness he called upon the Madonna with a series of meaningful and varied titles: dear little Mother, beautiful little Mother, beautiful Virgin Mary, most holy Mother, sweetest Mother, blessed Mother, tender Mother, most tender Mother, heavenly Mother, Consoler, Queen of Martyrs – all of which seem like the notes of a symphony.

The recollection of the numberless benefits that he had received graciously from the Virgin moved Padre Pio deeply. He spoke with evident pleasure and gratitude of her maternal care which 'pricks our pretensions'. He proclaimed that, thanks to her help, he was victorious over diabolic deceptions, and that through the guidance of her hand he had been able to come close to Jesus and enjoy his friendship. He regretted his inability to thank her and pay back her maternal care as he would have liked. He invited all creatures to love her, because she is truly worthy of being loved by all.

238 I wish I had a loud, loud voice so that I could invite all the world's sinners to love the Madonna. But because this is not within my power, I have asked my guardian angel to undertake this task for me (277).

239 Poor little Mother, how much you love me! This realisation has come to me afresh at the beginning of this beautiful month [of May]. How great was the care with which she accompanied me to the altar this morning! It seemed to me, as she filled my heart with holy affections, that I was the only thing she had to think about. I felt a mysterious fire in my heart, that I cannot understand. I felt the need to use ice to put out this fire, which is consuming me (276).

240 *Oh! le joli mois que le mois de mai! C'est le plus beau de l'année!*[32] Yes, my Father, this month speaks so eloquently of Mary's sweetness and beauty! When I think of the numberless good things that she has done for me, I am ashamed of myself because I have not loved her heart and her hand as I should, and through both she has, out of her goodness, shown me compassion. What distresses me the most is that in return for our Mother's affectionate care I have given her nothing but continual cause for indignation.

How many times have I confided the sorrowful anxieties of my troubled heart to this Mother! And how many times has she consoled me! But how do I acknowledge this?... In the greatest torments, I seemed no longer to have a mother on the earth but a most merciful one in heaven. But when my heart was at

---

32. 'Oh! what a beautiful month the month of May is! It is the most beautiful of the whole year!'

peace, I forgot nearly everything I owed the blessed heavenly Mother. I even almost forgot the debt of gratitude owed to this blessed heavenly Mother! ... The month of May is for me the month of graces (275).

241 Finally, the month of the beautiful little Mother has returned... This dear little Mother continues to lavish her maternal care on me, especially in this month. Her care of me concerns my pretensions... What have I done to merit such great care? I seem by my actions to live in a state of continual forgetfulness, forgetting not only of her Son, but also of the name of Christian that I bear. And yet this most tender Mother in her great mercy, wisdom and goodness decided to punish me in a very lofty way by pouring into my heart such graces and so many of them, that when I found myself in hers and Jesus' presence I felt impelled to cry out: 'Where am I, where have I come to? Who is that who is near me?' I feel myself burning without fire. I feel myself held and bound to the Son through this Mother without even seeing the chains that hold me so close. A thousand flames consume me. I feel I am dying continually and yet I live (357).

242 May Jesus and Mary continue to be parents to me. O my Father, who could tell you of the consolations that the heavenly little Mother gives me in this month [of May] (285).

243 'Abandon yourself', says Jesus, 'to my Heart and remember that I am Father especially of orphans. My Mother will make up for that other mother that I desired for myself' (505).

244 I am very much in debt to our common mother Mary for repelling the deceits of the enemy. I also thank this good Mother for such singular graces which she gives in every moment. Meanwhile, could you suggest to me some new way which would enable me to please this blessed Mother completely. The greatest sign of love that you could show me would be for you yourself to thank the Madonna on my behalf as well (224).

245 The only thing that displeases me, my Father, is that I do not have sufficient ways in which to thank our beautiful Virgin Mary. I do not doubt that it is by her intercession that I have received such strength from the Lord, as I bear with sincere resignation the many mortifications which I am subject to from day to day (182).

246 My spirit felt itself transported in a flash into an enormous room full of dazzling light. On a throne studded with precious jewels I saw a lady of rare beauty seated; the lady was the most holy Virgin and she had the child in her womb, and the child had a majestic bearing and a face that shone more radiantly than the sun. Around them there was a great multitude of angels in very splendid forms (388).

247 Now it seems that I can understand what the martyrdom of our sweetest Mother was; I had not been able to do so before. Oh, if humankind were able to understand this torment! Who would be able to suffer with our dear co-redemptrix? Who would refuse her the beautiful title of Queen of Martyrs? (384).

248 May the sorrowful Virgin obtain for us her Son's permission to enter ever more deeply into the mystery of the Cross and together with her rejoice in Jesus' sufferings. The most certain proof of love is to suffer for the beloved, and so, since the Son of God suffered such sorrows for pure love, there is no doubt that the Cross he bore has become as loveable as love itself (602).

249 O God, I feel such agony in the depths of my heart! When will it settle? I feel my heart being torn to pieces. I have nowhere to rest it. If only I could at least have the satisfaction of relieving this inner martyrdom through tears! The suffering is great, and it has turned me to stone.

Now, O Jesus, I understand why your Mother, gazing at you on the Cross, did not cry. But tell me, O Jesus, what ever is this inner voice that I hear continually, 'Ubi est Deus tuus?'[33] I cannot reply to it for fear of lying (993).

250 The strength of Satan, who assaults me, is terrible. But long live God! for he has placed my salvation and the ultimate victory in the hands of our heavenly Mother. Protected and guided by such a tender Mother, I will stay to fight as long as God wishes – secure and full of confidence in this Mother that I will never succumb.

How far away, O Father, does the hope for victory seem when seen from the land of exile! But how close and how sure it seems when it is seen from the house of God, where one remains under the protection of this most holy Mother! (576).

---

33. 'Where is your God?'

251 I come now to ask you for a permission, and I hope that you will not refuse it. In the honour of the Virgin I wish to vow to abstain from eating fruit every Wednesday. There seems to me there is no danger to my health in this. But I leave it to you to decide (390).

252 May the most holy Virgin obtain love for us through crosses, sufferings and sorrows. She was the first to follow the Gospel in all its fullness, in all its severity, even before it was made public; may she obtain the same for us, and may she herself give us the impetus to come immediately into her presence (602).

253 Let us strive also, like many chosen souls have done, to follow behind this blessed Mother, to walk always in her presence; for there is no other road that leads to life than the one taken by our Mother. We who wish to arrive at the destination, let us not refuse to take this road (602).

254 May the Mother of Jesus, and our Mother, obtain for us from her Son the grace to live a life according to the heart of God, a life that is entirely interior and hidden in him. May this dear Mother unite us so closely to Jesus that we will never be taken or led astray by anything in this world here below. May she keep us always in the presence of infinite lovingness, in the presence of Jesus; only then will we be able to call ourselves with Paul, sons of God in the midst of a sinful and corrupt people (606).

255 I wish I could fly and invite all creatures to love Jesus and to love Mary (357).

256 May she who entered the world without stain, obtain for us from her Son the grace to leave this world without fault (514).

IX

CHURCH, PRIESTHOOD AND EUCHARIST

Church, Priesthood and Eucharist form, so to speak, a triptych, each part linked to the others by an invisible link. Invisible though it be, this link is nonetheless easily recognisable.

Padre Pio was a most beloved son of Christ's Church, a priest according to the divine Heart and an impassioned lover of Jesus in the Eucharist.

In his daily prayer and in the suffering he sought and accepted, Padre Pio had the needs 'of the holy Church, our most tender mother' continually present. He participated deeply in the Church's sorrows and joys, he rejoiced in her triumphs and feared the dangers that threatened her.

Those fortunate enough to assist him while he celebrated the Mass, will never forget his expression of unutterable suffering and blessed recollection. All were able to sense his intense personal participation in the sacrifice of the divine victim; but the intimate, energetic and intense work of his soul, filled with suffering and love, remained hidden from the eyes of the faithful. Not even Padre Pio himself could find adequate terms to explain all this to his directors. It should be noted that some of the more remarkable mystical phenomena experienced by Padre Pio, such as substantial touches (a type of communication from God), the gift of tears, the fusion of hearts, the stigmata and so on, appeared in conjunction with the celebration of the Mass.

Daily Mass was his greatest comfort and the comfort he desired most. The deprivation of daily Mass was his greatest suffering.

Padre Pio was devoured by a hunger and thirst to fill himself with the spotless flesh of the divine Lamb. The Eucharistic union produced marvellous effects in him. He would never have wished to separate himself from the sacramental presence of Jesus. He counselled and promoted daily communion and deplored the negligence and indifference with which this sacrament of love is sometimes treated.

The Friar from Pietrelcina felt the responsibility of his priestly vocation so strongly that he condemned very vigorously those priests whose conduct saddened and betrayed the Heart of Christ, his principal accusation being their negligence in promoting the Eucharistic worship. Following the exhortation of his Spiritual director, he rejoiced to offer his heavy cross 'for the many brother priests who are not concerned with the delicate and holy nature of the ministry, and who suffer greatly on account of its inherent trials' (1272).

257 May infinite thanks be offered to the merciful Jesus, who has wiped away the tears of his Church and who has consoled her widowhood by sending his Head [the new Pope]; all has gone as the heart of God willed it. Let us offer the new Pontiff our most sincere best wishes, may he truly be a worthy successor of that great Pope, Pius X, a truly noble and holy soul; Rome never had another equal to him.

Born of the people, he never denied his humble background. He was truly the peerlessly good shepherd, the most peaceful king, the sweet and meek Jesus on earth. Oh! we will remember the good Pontiff more because we have an intercessor with the Most High than because we wish to send our fervent prayers to heaven for the repose of his great soul.

He was the first, the greatest and the most innocent victim of the fratricidal war that deafened Europe with weapons and soldiers, and filled it with terror. He was not able to resist the unleashing of the terrifying storm any more, and his heart, that all his life had been a fountain of an apostolate of peace for the whole world, was wrenched apart in a spasm of pain. The world now misses him because of the great love that burnt in his breast (493).

258 While all this happened I had time to offer my entire self to the Lord, for the same end that the Holy Father had in mind when he recommended that the whole Church make an offering of prayer and sacrifice. I had not even finished doing this, when I felt myself falling into this most hard prison and I heard its door closing with a bang behind me. I felt myself bound by the hardest of chains, and I immediately felt my life failing me. From that moment I have felt myself in hell, without a break, not even for an instant (1053).

259 May the unborn Child grant my weak and feeble prayers, the prayers that I will address to him with greater holy insistence in these days on behalf of the Order, Superiors, the Province and the whole Church (443).

260 Let us pray, my Father, that the Lord will disperse the dense clouds that are gathering on the Church's horizon (318).

261 Let us pray for the Holy Church, our most tender mother. Let us consecrate and sacrifice everything to God for this end. Meanwhile let us wait expectantly (466).

⁓❦⁓

262 Do you know, my Father, to where my thoughts are flying as I write? To the beautiful day of my feast. Tomorrow, the Feast of St Lawrence, is the day of my feast too. I have already begun to feel the joy of that sacred day again. Since yesterday evening I have begun to taste paradise... And what will it be like when we enjoy it eternally?

I have been comparing the peace of heart that I experienced on that day to the peace of heart that I have begun to experience since the vigil, and I find no difference.

On St Lawrence's day my heart was more on fire with love for Jesus. How happy I was! How much I enjoyed that day!

Read this letter, Father, and since I do not doubt that you love me, give thanks to Jesus and pray to him, on my behalf (297).

263 What gives me the most sorrow is not being able to either celebrate [the Eucharist], or fill myself with the spotless body of the divine Lamb. *Fiat!* (955).

264 Be consoled, dear Father, by the sweet thought that you love Jesus, and that you are loved very much by him. Let us ask for grace with the Spouse of the sacred Canticle: 'O that he would kiss me with the kisses of his mouth. For your love is better than wine!'[34] How often Jesus gives us this kiss of peace in the most holy sacrament, especially to us priests. Yes, let us ardently desire this kiss from the divine mouth, and, even more, let us show that we are grateful for it. What dearer gift can we wretched mortals desire from God? (406).

265 I still at times feel tempted to discontinue daily communion, but I have always managed to master myself. May all be to the glory of God. How could I, my Father, live without drawing close to receive Jesus, even for a single morning? (186).

266 I weep and I groan at the feet of Jesus in the sacrament because of this. Many times it seems I am comforted, but it also seems that sometimes Jesus hides himself from my soul. The pen is powerless to describe what goes on in my soul in these moments when Jesus has so hidden himself. When I draw close to the most holy communion, the evil deceiver assails me with doubts as to whether I have been successful in repelling temptation. There are, my Father, moments of intense battle. And Oh! what strength I must use against myself, so that I don't deprive myself of the comfort provided by the Eucharist (187).

267 But what wounds me most of all, my Father, is the thought of Jesus in the sacrament. My heart feels as if it is drawn by a greater strength before uniting itself to him each morning in the sacrament. I have such a hunger and thirst before I

---

34. Song 1:2.

receive him that I almost die from anxiety. And precisely because I am unable not to unite myself to him, I am constrained even when very ill to go and nourish myself with his flesh.

And this hunger and thirst is not satisfied when I have received him in the sacrament, but grows even greater. When I have this highest God in my possession, when the fullness of the sweetness is really great, I am almost ready to say to Jesus: 'Enough! I can barely take any more!' I almost forget that I am in the world. My heart and mind do not desire anything anymore, and for long stretches of time I am not actually capable of desiring other things (217).

268 Sometimes I ask myself if there could be any souls who do not feel a divine fire burning in their breasts, especially when they stand before him in the Sacrament. This seems impossible to me, particularly if the souls in question are priests or religious. Perhaps those souls who say that they do not feel this fire, do not notice it because of the greatness of their hearts. Only a benign interpretation such as this prevents me from distancing myself from them and accusing them of shameful untruth (317).

269 I have many things to tell you, but words fail me. All I can tell you is that my heart beats very strongly when I am with Jesus in the Sacrament. It seems at times to want to come out of my breast.

I feel sometimes such an enkindling at the altar that I cannot describe it. My face feels almost ready to burst into flames. What signs these might be, my Father, I do not know (234).

270 I am deeply moved when I consider the great things that the Lord is doing in that privileged soul. But unfortunately, the dangers surrounding that treasure of graces and evangelical purity are also many! Therefore the best and only way for it to stay faithful to God – being almost continually in contact with people without faith and without law and who have blasphemy always on their lips and the hatred of God in their hearts – is to draw near daily to receive Jesus at the table of the angels (362).

271 It [the soul] must never neglect to fill itself with the food of the angels. It will be frequently tempted by the enemy, who is not ignorant of the profit that the soul receives from this food, and the profit many others in turn will receive through it. But it shouldn't be afraid. Jesus promises that he will never cease to help it; Jesus' promise is constant, and he only fails in what he promises when the soul becomes unfaithful (379).

272 'It is a soul', says Jesus, 'that is very dear to me! Tell it that work, withdrawal, prayer and attendance at the sacraments will satisfy it' (505).

273 Yesterday, on the Feast of St Joseph, only God knows how much sweetness I experienced, especially after the Mass, so much so that I still feel it now. My head and my heart were burning; but with a fire that was doing me good. My mouth experienced all the sweetness of the spotless flesh of the Son of God. Oh, if only in this moment when I still feel almost everything, I could find a way to hold these consolations for ever in my heart – I would undoubtedly be in paradise! (265).

274 I have never participated in such a holy ceremony as the one that took place on the day I was confirmed. I weep in my heart with consolation during this holy ceremony, because I recall what the most holy Paraclete made me feel on the day I received the sacrament of confirmation – a unique day which I will remember all my life. How many sweet emotions the consoling Spirit made me feel on that day! At the thought of that day I feel myself burning with a most intense flame, that burns, consumes and yet is not painful (471).

275 Because I am very [too?] weak, I don't have the heart to implore our heavenly Father to take his beloved Son from the world and so remove him from all the outrages he suffers. What would humanity be without Christ in its midst? And more particularly, what would become of me? I feel all my weakness and powerlessness. I tremble at this sorrowful thought and I am seized by the horror and fear of the punishments that God could send our unfortunate brothers. '*Fervet opus*'[35], my beloved Father. Let us beg our good Father that he doesn't punish *ad perditionen* (414).

276 In this frame of mind I received your letter this morning. I opened it in haste in the hope of finding some comfort there. But what did I find! As soon as I read the first lines full of reproofs, my spirits ebbed away even more. I was about to vest myself to celebrate the Mass, but I had to leave the sacristy to stifle my bitterness with tears. In the celebration of the holy Mass, right at the moment of

---

35. Virgil, *Georgics*, IV, 169: 'all aglow is the work'

consecration, Jesus comforted me a little, and then it all began again (1234).

277 What on earth is all of this? My day began on the twenty-ninth of May and has not yet drawn to a close. I feel morally and physically crushed. It seems that the only time that I am not conscious of it all in its terrifying display, is when I am exercising my ministry.

So melancholy, besieged, wearisome and sighing I draw near to the altar, in loathing and aversion on account of the fury that accompanies me, the monstrosity and ugliness. What happens in that tremendous time when I am at the altar, I am not able to tell you, because my soul feels it but does not perceive it.

How come? Could this be evidence of a sacrilegious kiss, when one's life feels itself to be sighing and bleeding, and one's vital essence gives signs that one might be truly condemned to hell? More often than not I couldn't tell you if I was truly involved in the loftiness of the act* or not: torpor seems to accompany me before and then swallow me up after.

Oh God, if I were to think this, my life would fold up in that instant. At other times the merest indication was enough to make me collapse over the altar. This lethargic weariness, which derives from my utter powerlessness, was for the most part extremely tormenting. Because I made such furious efforts to counteract it, the lethargy was almost always followed by the complete freezing of the inner and outer senses of the body (1040).

---

* Translator's Note: This probably means that Padre Pio is wondering whether he is celebrating mass in a way acceptable to God.

278 For a number of days I have begun to hope that Jesus does not want to deprive me of this one comfort that remains to me (941).

279 Here another ten days have gone past. May the divine Will be done! I hope that all will end well. I am extremely distressed for the single reason that I cannot celebrate [the Mass], because there is no chapel here and we are not allowed to leave. I am desolate! May it please God to bring me quickly out of this dark prison [the military clinic] (932).

280 I won't speak to you about my physical state. It isn't the subject of our discussion, and I don't really worry about it at all, and I also want it to be this way for you. I will only tell you that Jesus leaves me the comfort of celebrating Mass every day. But if he wishes to deprive me of this also, *fiat*! (753).

281 That awful beast is convinced that he cannot have (that soul) for himself, and so, unfortunately, not being able to have it any more, he strives wholeheartedly to have a lesser thing – to prevent it reaching a greater perfection. What concerns me is that it would have need of a director who is well enlightened in the ways of God. But where can you find such a one in these dreadful times? Even the most faithful Jesus lamented about this. Oh, in what sorrowful times have we come to know each other! Yet again the Son of God raises the bitter lament from his divine Heart: 'The harvest is plentiful, but the labourers are few'[36] (533).

---

36. Mt 9:37; Lk 10:2.

282 Hear, my Father, the just complaint of our sweetest Jesus: 'I remain alone in the churches, by day and by night. They do not bother with the sacrament of the altar any more. And even those who do speak of it, alas! with what indifference and coldness they speak' (342).

283 'My Heart', says Jesus, 'has been forgotten. No one is concerned with my love anymore. I am continually saddened. My house has become for many a place of entertainment. This is so even for my ministers, whom I have always regarded with favour, whom I have loved like the apple of my eye: these should comfort my heart filled with bitterness and help me to redeem souls. But who would believe it? That from them I should receive ingratitude and a refusal to acknowledge me. I see, my son, many of them who… (here he grew quiet, the sobs caught in his throat, and he wept in secret)… under hypocritical appearances betray me with sacrilegious communions, treading underfoot the light and strength that I continually give them…'. Jesus continued to complain. My Father, how bad it makes me feel to see Jesus weep! Have you experienced it yet? (342).

284 On Friday morning [28 March 1913] I was still in bed, when Jesus appeared to me. He was all melancholy and disfigured. He showed me a great multitude of regular and secular priests, among whom there were different ecclesiastical dignitaries. Some were celebrating [Mass], some were vesting, and others were taking their sacred vestments off.

The face of Jesus in distress pained me greatly, and so I asked him why he was suffering so much. But I got no reply. However, his gaze went back to those priests. Shortly after, almost horrified and as if he was tired of looking, he turned his gaze away and lifted it towards me. To my great horror, I noticed that two tears were running down his cheek. He moved away from the mob of priests and looking greatly sickened he cried out: 'Butchers!'.

He turned to me and said: 'My son, do not believe that my agony lasted only three hours, no. I will be in agony until the end of the world because of the very souls that have benefited most from me. During the time of my agony, my son, you must not sleep. My soul searches around for a drop or two of human compassion; but, alas! they leave me alone under the burden of indifference. Ingratitude and the greatest of my ministers render my agony terrible indeed. Alas, how badly they respond to my love! What distresses me even more is when some add scorn or unbelief to indifference. How many times was I about to strike them down, but was held back by the guardian angels and those souls that love me... Write to your Father and tell him what you have seen and heard from me this morning. Tell him to show your letter to Father Provincial...'.

Jesus went on, but I cannot reveal what he said to any creature in this world. This apparition caused such pain in my body, and even greater pain in my soul, that for the entire day I was prostrate and I believed I would have died of it if the sweetest Jesus had not already revealed to me... Jesus has good reason unfortunately to complain of our ingratitude! (350).

285 Continue, continue, O Father, to devote all your strength to the salvation of others, because this is exactly what Jesus wants from you. Humble yourself beneath the powerful hand of the

Lord in the time of trial, so that you will be worthy to be exalted when he comes to you. Stay calm, however, because the Lord is with you and there is nothing to fear (532).

286 I promise you that I will not cease to use sweet force with the Heart of the divine Spouse, so that he might give you light to safely guide the souls that are entrusted to you (485).

287 May Jesus and Mary help you always, and always give your word the ability to convert souls and arrest the progress of those who run along the road to ruin. May it be so (535).

288 Do it, I beg you, O Father. It will do you much good. We can never work too hard to save a soul! (543).

289 Don't become heartbroken regarding certain individuals, because their hearts have become entirely insensitive. Divine mercy does not soften them; kindness and favour does not attract them; with sweetness they become insolent, they rage against severity and in adversity they despair. Deaf, blind, insensitive to what could shake them up, the greatest warnings and the greatest exhortations serve only to double their darkness and confirm them in their hardness. Is there any more monstrous darkness than this? May the divine Master touch their hearts and convert them! (654).

X

GUIDE OF SOULS

In any consideration of the Spiritual life, direction occupies an important place. This chapter clearly illustrates this importance. Due to a number of providential circumstances, Padre Pio became, through his correspondence with those he recognised as unquestioned and authoritative directors of his own soul, the sure and illuminated guide of the very same directors; we have many indications of how he undertook this difficult, delicate and demanding task and this allows us to see how he approached it. A brief summary of the principal elements of this approach may be helpful: he possessed the knowledge that he was transmitting principles and practices drawn not from human knowledge or cold and abstract reason, but precisely and principally from personal experiences and from the deepest divine movements in his own soul. He was thus able to give clear and precise directions, certain and definite decisions, and the inspired application of general principles to individual, personal and concrete cases – he was clear, sincere and frank, whether in reproof, advising or encouraging; he participated in a lively and heartfelt manner in others' anxieties, griefs, crosses and difficulties, as well as in their joys and personal progress on the path to goodness. Moreover, among all the other qualities that emerge from his teaching and which rendered his direction particularly successful and effective, we should note his singular gifts for discovering diabolical deception, pointing out the action of grace and the reality of divine partiality, and the calming of souls shaken and troubled by doubts, uncertainties and temptations.

It would be impossible here to document all of these remarkable characteristics. We will therefore limit ourselves to illustrate the particular charism he was given of exhorting his listeners to peace of soul, to the tranquillity necessary for progress on the path to goodness and to a calmness in all of life's ups and downs. We chose this subject because of the importance accorded to it by masters of the Spiritual life, and because of the insistence and variety of ways in which Padre Pio returns to it in his correspondence with his directors.

❧

290 Peace is simplicity of spirit, serenity of mind, tranquillity of soul, the bond of love.

Peace is order, it is harmony in each one of us. It is the continual rejoicing that is born from the testimony of a good conscience. It is the holy joyfulness of the heart in which God reigns.

Peace is the way of perfection; or rather, in peace one finds perfection.

And the devil, who knows all this very well, makes every effort to make us lose our peace (607).

291 We will never advance a single step in this virtue [gospel simplicity], unless we try to live in a holy and unchanging peace. Sweet is the yoke of Jesus, light his burden, therefore we should give the enemy no space to worm his way into our hearts in order to take this peace from us (607).

292 The enemy of our salvation knows only too well that peace of heart is a sure sign of divine help, and so he misses no opportunity to make us lose it. For this reason, we must always be on the alert in this matter. Jesus will help us (603).

293 May the glory of our heavenly Father be that which holds you always at the ready to protect yourself from the blows of the enemy. Do not give in, I beg you, my Father, to the storms of Satan, because Jesus is telling you that in this new struggle he will not permit the enemy to touch your spirit at all (485).

294 We have raised our thoughts to heaven, our true homeland, of which the earth is only a pale reflection. With divine assistance we strive to preserve, in every event, joyful or sad, that serenity and calm that become the true followers of the fair-haired Nazarene (596).

295 Let us be on the alert never to become troubled by any ominous mishaps that might befall us; such disturbance can never be separated from imperfection, as it always has its origin in selfishness and self-love. The more agitated our hearts are, the more frequent and direct are the assaults of the enemy. Our enemy takes advantage of our natural weakness, which hinders us from following the straight path of virtue (603).

296 Let us be on the look-out for even the slightest symptom of anxiety, and as soon as we notice that we have fallen into discouragement let us turn to God with a child's trust and total abandonment.

Every disturbance displeases Jesus, because such disturbances are never unaccompanied by imperfection and they always have their origin in selfishness and self-love (608).

297 Put to rest, I beg you, beloved Father, your anxieties regarding your spirit, because they seem to be a true waste of time in our dealings with eternity; and what is worse, because of these many anxieties – which can be holy in themselves – and our fragility and the powerful whisperings of the devil, all our good actions are always, if you will allow me the expression, soiled by some measure of lack of confidence in God's goodness (405).

298 May the flames of divine love consume in you all that does not know Jesus. May the divine Spirit strengthen you always with new courage through his grace, to confront with tranquillity and peace the war which comes to us from our enemies (596).

299 The soul should grieve over one thing only: offending God, and even on this point we must be very cautious. We must of course be very sorry for our failings, but with a peaceful sorrow, always trusting in divine mercy (608).

300 And so, O Father, the bitterness of the trial is sweetened by the balm of God's goodness and mercy. Long live God! who alternates the joys and tears so wonderfully that he leads the soul by unknown ways to the attainment of perfection – the perfection that he knows how to draw out even from that soul which seems to be evil and is reputed to be so.

Perfection is the flower that the merciful God makes blossom between the thorns of suffering, watered by the tears of the soul that suffers patiently, that conforms humbly to divine wishes and prays fervently and warmly (595).

301 If we keep our spirit tranquil and in peace in every difficult situation, we will do well in the ways of the Lord. On the contrary, if we lose this peace, our every effort at attaining eternal life will yield little or no fruit (608).

302 Moreover, let us guard ourselves against certain types of self-reproof and self-remorse. These reproofs more often than not come from the enemy, intended to disturb the peace we have in God.

If such reproofs and remorse humble us and make us diligent in performing good actions, without taking our faith in God from us, then we can be sure they come from God. But if they confuse us and render us fearful, suspicious, lazy, slow to do good, then we can be sure they come from the devil and, as such, we should banish them by taking shelter in trust in God (608).

303 Calm yourself, O Father. Don't pay any attention to these vain and useless fears. Fill the emptiness of your heart with an ardent love for Jesus. Humble yourself always beneath the powerful hand of God, always accepting the tribulations that he sends us with serenity of spirit and humility of heart, so that when he comes to visit us he will exalt us by giving us his grace. Cast all your cares onto him, because he cares for us more than a mother cares for her baby (597).

304 Courage, then, my good Father. Live in tranquillity. Jesus will assist you always. Better exile and the will of God, than the tents of Jacob [the cloister] without it (891).

305 Do not let the thought that the time of trial is still long, preoccupy you. It is better to suffer purgatory through the will of God than to delight in the cloister, which is a pale reflection of the heavenly Jerusalem. One cannot reach salvation without crossing the stormy sea, which continually threatens ruin (829).

306 I perceive in you a little agitation and care that are hampering your latest efforts to be patient. '*In patientia vestra possidebitis anima vestras*'[37], our divine Master tells us. Thus it is through patience that we possess our souls. And in the measure that our patience is perfect, so the possession of our souls will be complete, perfect and sure. Therefore the less our patience is mixed with cares and anxieties, the more it will be perfect (890).

307 Do not cease trying to make them fully understand how important it is not to grieve ourselves over the ups and downs of life, because this always leads to the heart's confidence in God diminishing, instead of expanding (419).

308 Do not let them become at all worried by this business, because worrying always lowers our spirits. Worry, depending on the degree to

---

37. Lk 21:19: 'By your patience you will possess your souls', Latin Vulgate

which it affects us, diminishes charity in the heart and confidence in God. This is no small thing, because it prevents the Spirit from acting upon the heart in an unhindered manner (434).

309 One should entrust oneself entirely to the sweetest Spouse of souls. Let them lay their heads on the Heart of this most tender Spouse, whose beloved disciples they are. Let them not fear the clamour of the unbelieving mob, because the heavenly Master will not allow a hair of their head to be harmed, as he did not allow any harm to come to his disciples in Gethsemane. Unobserved by the insolent rabble they ascend with the King to the summit of Calvary (434).

310 Your laments and fears, I repeat, neither have their beginning in God, nor is he their author. It is Satan who places such fully-formed fears in your hearts, and God has permitted this so that you may become perfect. But God wants you to be scornful and bear this trial in peace. The more you complain, the more you try to reject these trials, the longer they will last. You must resign yourself to letting things be, even when it isn't granted to you to let things be. Jesus is very happy with you; what have you to be afraid of, then? (1203).

311 [Your brief letter] distressed me because I see how much you are suffering; suffering caused by silly and ridiculous things. Scorn them, for heaven's sake, and give them not weight, if you don't want to play the enemy's game (1198).

312 You complain because you are tried again and again in the same way. Well, well,

Father, what have you to be afraid of? Of the divine Creator, who wants to perfect his masterpiece in this way? Do you want to leave in the hands of such a magnificent craftsman only a simple roughed-out piece of work? If so, you really are a dilettante when it comes to perfect works! (1195)

313 Jesus wants you to know that the various Spiritual sorrows that upset you so much, are willed directly by him to test you and not to castigate you, to purify you even more and render you, as far as is possible, like him. He is the prototype of every soul that has chosen the best part, of divine service. He wants you, as a sign of gratitude, to be more docile to these divine workings he is performing (643).

314 I am most sorry to hear that Satan has once again seized you. But do not fear, Jesus and Mary are with you and nothing evil will befall you (1241).

315 Live with a tranquil spirit, because you have nothing to fear. Jesus permits a spirit to struggle not to punish it, but to purify it. The trial is not death, but salvation (878).

316 Keep yourself from continually converting your occupations into disturbances and anxieties of spirit. Even if you are being tossed around on the waves and blown about by the winds of many perplexities, look up constantly and say to our Lord: 'O God, it is for you that I row and for you I sail; you are my guide and my helmsman!' (842).

317 Try your best to hurry them up [your affairs], one after another, as you best can manage. Employ your spirit faithfully in them, but with sweetness and gentleness. If God grants you success, bless him for it; if it doesn't please him to grant it, bless him equally. It should be enough for you to strive with a willing spirit to accomplish your tasks, because the Lord and reason itself do not require results of you, but application, commitment and the necessary diligence; such things depend on you, but not success (992).

318 Strive to conquer and subdue this excessive fear of yours, otherwise, Father, Jesus will not smile on you (825).

319 I pray you, my good Father, to be tranquil and resigned in all things. Jesus is with you and is happy with you. I never cease to plead with the divine Heart on your behalf, so that he may give you ever more grace to sustain and fight the good fight. Do not doubt it, victory will smile on you, and will certainly be yours (1233).

320 Do not tire yourself out searching for God outside, because he is within you, he is with you, he is in your groans, he is in your searching. I exhort you, for as long as this trial lasts, to act in complete conformity with God's wishes, and to imitate Isaac when in the hands of Abraham and to hope with both of them 'contra spem'.[38] Do not fear, my dear Father, and believe me, what I have just told you comes from Jesus (1210).

---

38. Rom 4:18: 'against hope'.

321 Courage, my dear Father, Jesus is with you and victory will smile on you for certain (1130).

322 Live in tranquillity and rest yourself on the divine Heart, without any fear, because those who have been corrected through trials, are safe from divine justice (825).

323 Strive to control the anxieties of your heart. Have confidence in the great work of your own sanctification and that of others and be calm. Leave the rest to Jesus (769).

324 What ever is this excessive worry that you have about that worn-out soul of yours? Calm yourself, and with calmness you won't be kept waiting long for it. Is this the road that leads the elect to heaven? Isn't the spring more charming and surprising when winter has been bleak and stormy? Well then! my good Father, leave your fears behind and let the divine doctor get to work, even in the guise of a surgeon (905).

325 Live in tranquillity for all that regards your spirit. Continue offering the sacrifice of your life to the Lord, and all that you are enduring, and Jesus will continue to reign in your heart like the true sovereign he is. To make yourself ever more worthy of the glory of the blessed, offer all that you are enduring to God a hundred times a day and more. Hold yourself out to him with a loving will (906).

326 There is nothing that could or should dry up the milk and honey of charity – regret, troubles or low spirits. Therefore, among these children of the homeland live in holy joy. Offer them Spiritual comfort, with a good and gracious appearance, so that they come running to you with joy. I'm not saying, my dear Father, that you should be false in any way, but sweet, gentle and amiable. In short, love with a heartfelt love, fatherly and caring for these poor unfortunates of the world, and you will have done everything, and you will be everything to everyone, father to each one, helping all. This by itself is sufficient (974).

327 Do not ever allow your soul to become sad, nor live in bitterness of spirit or scruples. Because he who loved you and died that you might live is sweet, good and loveable (927).

328 I observe another thing in you that should not be considered as something of little weight. When the Lord tries you through aridity, you often lose some of your tranquillity and you reluctantly submit to the trial. You give yourself a thousand worries, when there is no real need to, because even in this state of trial you can possess true devotion and true love of God.

You would know very well, if you paused to examine yourself, that even in this state you possess that general inclination and willingness of spirit to do what you know and understand to be pleasing to God. And surely such a willingness is the inner witness which ought to be enough to convince us that our souls are very close to God and not rejected by him? (991).

329 There is another imperfection in you. It is the great variety and difficulty of your undertakings, and not the unhappy results of your efforts, that often produce anxieties in your spirit. And such anxieties are nothing other than impatience and resentment, all things that displease God's majesty (991).

330 I am delighted to hear that you are calm in your spirit. The only thing I don't like is that little something of breathless eagerness in your aspirations. Jesus, as it was he who told me about it, will, I hope, give you the strength to correct it (1255).

331 Your preoccupation that you will have to encounter a severe divine judge is caused by none other than the enemy. Banish this temptation always, together with the other, namely the matter that seems so evident to you. The matter that gives rise to a judgement, is created by Satan, and from Satan himself comes the light that makes the same seem to be indisputable. This is the only truth and all the truth (1130).

332 I recommend calm, and again calm. Deep anxiety dries up Christian devotion, and renders it sterile (1260).

333 Be courageous. The trial will last for a long time; but purgatory, when one suffers for the love of God, is sweet. It will pass, Father, and endless spring will come, the richer in beauty the harder the storms were. Courage, then, and keep moving forward (822).

XI

THE SCHOOL OF VIRTUE

It would be almost impossible to present a complete collection of the passages in Padre Pio's correspondence that deal with Christian virtue. Sometimes these references to virtue are fleeting allusions. Such allusions are certainly very important and significant, but because of their fragmentary nature it is not easy to detach them from their context and present them as thoughts in their own right. And on the other hand, some virtues find their logical place in other chapters of this anthology.

Therefore we will present a simple mosaic formed from a series of passages which touch on the following virtues: faith, hope, charity, humility, obedience, simplicity, confidence in God, gratitude, sweetness... To illustrate some of these virtues more clearly we have included passages that touch on their opposite: pride, arrogance, vainglory, impatience...

Many of these passages contain exhortations to souls regarding proper conduct, and reasons for such conduct – but all reflect genuine practice and lived experience, words and ideas incarnated in a life. The master speaks and teaches, but, even without wishing it, he commands admiration and imitation.

334 Regarding what you have asked me, I don't want to say anything more concerning your spirit than this: remain tranquil, striving ever more

intensely with divine help to keep humility and charity firm within you, for they are the most important parts of the great building, and all the others depend on them. Keep yourself firmly fixed in them. One is the highest thing, the other the lowest. The preservation of the entire building depends on both the foundations and the roof. If we keep our hearts applied to the constant exercise of these [virtues], we will encounter no difficulties with the others. They are the mothers of the virtues; the other virtues follow them like chicks follow their mother (1139).

335 Above all you should have charity very much at heart, charity towards God, your neighbour and yourself. Refrain from judging anyone, save when you have to do so through the discharge of duty. In this way you will maintain respect for all, and you will show yourself to be a worthy child of our heavenly Father who causes the sun to shine on the just and the sinner (1134).

336 I have such respect for others that, since the Lord has been continually enriching me with such treasures, I am always moved to judge others' actions in a favourable light. This I do because I believe that all love the Lord more than I do. If sometimes I have to restrain myself somewhat regarding such actions, it is for a few moments only, and I never allow myself to form a set judgement about them, even though I see the thing very clearly (429).

337 Such is the opinion I have of myself, that I don't know if there be any worse than me. And when I see in others certain things that appear to be sins, I cannot persuade myself that those who have

committed them have offended God, even though I see the thing itself very clearly. General wickedness alone worries me, and it very often saddens me greatly (423).

338 Be lenient with all, especially with those who have consecrated themselves without reserve to Jesus and to souls (1243).

339 May the divine Master inform you of my true present state. He shows me compassion. Will my entire life be enough, my Father, to thank the goodness of our heavenly Father for the continuous and singular favours that he grants to those who continually offend him? May this our good God be blessed, who does not know how to punish this poor soul in any way but by inflicting on it an ever-growing indigestion of Spiritual consolations (537).

340 My monstrousness appears disgusting in my own eyes, as it does in the eyes of the God of purity and those of every person. I loathe and hate myself, especially because I do not know the way in which I can escape this monstrousness. Father, I am unworthy to utter this name and address you with my pitiful utterings (1096).

341 My God! I come to you in profound confusion; to you who are that which you are... I... nothing, wretched, worthy only of your scorn and pity. But... I reflect that I am dealing with the God who is mine. Ah! yes, and who can rival him? (1105).

342 My soul is totally preoccupied with the clear picture of its wretchedness! My God! how can I stand such a sorrowful sight; withdraw your

reflected ray of light from me, because I am not able to withstand the clear contrast it presents to me. My Father, in the light of his splendour I see all my own wickedness and ingratitude. I see the bad old man, crouched inside myself; he seems to want to repay God tit for tat for being absent, denying God his rights, which are some of this old man's strict duties. And what strength it requires to get him up onto his feet! My God! come quickly to my aid, because I fear for myself, faithless and ungrateful creature; protect me from my powerful enemies! (1090).

343 I see myself exactly as I am, and such knowledge leads me to recognise myself as undeserving of any attention, divine or human. I am descending already into the abyss of my deformity; and this dwelling-place has made me understand what awaits me.

Stop, my Father, stop, for heaven's sake, casting precious pearls before this unclean animal that doesn't know how to make use of them, nor to give them their true value. Acorns, and what is disgusting and fit only to be thrown away, are the only things that should be given to this coarse animal (1052).

344 I feel myself overwhelmed when faced with the Lord's many kindnesses to this wretched creature. And because I cannot find anything in myself that might have attracted the Lord to work so clearly in my soul, the following idea comes often into my mind: perhaps God in punishment for my infidelities (which are amongst other things, my Father, numberless) will not pay me back in this life, but will deprive me, and this completely justifiable, of his kingdom?

Perhaps this idea is a bit rash, but it is more credible if you take into account what my life once was (531).

345 Could a soul ever, forgetting its dignity and its lofty destination, carry its ingratitude so far as to raise its proud forehead against a most dear Lover? Alas! what a terrible revenge the very greatness of divine benefits must call on the heads of those who are ungrateful!

The Lord is able to protect us from such a horrendous misfortune – into which it seems I fall very often – and may he do so (655).

346 This is how that soul was captured by the devil in his nets. The soul seeing itself so favoured by God and close to his divine Heart, began to admire all the good that God had done, and saw clearly the difference between the goods of heaven and those of earth.

Up to here, it did well. But the enemy, who is always vigilant, seeing such great delight, began to insinuate in it a great confidence and certainty that it would never fall from this state of great enjoyment. He put in the soul such a clear vision of the heavenly reward, that it seemed impossible to ever renounce such a great happiness for things as physical and shameful as worldly pleasures.

The enemy used this misplaced confidence to make the soul lose that holy mistrust of itself. Such holy mistrust should never leave a soul, however privileged by God it might be.

Having lost, then, this mistrust of itself, little by little, the soul wretchedly threw itself into dangers, persuaded that it no longer had anything to fear for itself. This was the beginning, therefore, it was the cause of its final ruin.

What remains for us to do? Let us pray that the Lord place the soul on a good path. Let us pray unceasingly so that he might look on it as one previously of his own house, which ate his own bread (376).

347 This vice [vainglory] is more to be feared because it does not have a corresponding virtue that can be used to combat it. In fact, every vice has its remedy and its corresponding virtue: anger is defeated through meekness, envy through charity, pride with humility, and so on. Only vainglory has no corresponding virtue to combat it. It creeps into the most holy of acts. If you don't become aware of it, pride can entrench its camp in humility itself (397).

348 Vainglory is a special enemy of the souls that have consecrated themselves to the Lord and have given themselves to the Spiritual life. For this reason we can aptly call it the worm inside the souls of those who move towards perfection. It has been called the woodworm of holiness by the saints (396).

349 All the other vices prevail over only those who allow themselves to be conquered and dominated by them; but vainglory raises its head against those very persons who fight and conquer it. Vainglory is able to assault those who have conquered it through the very victories that these same conquerors won against it. It is an enemy that never grows weak; it is an enemy that fights against us in all the things we do, and unless we realise this we become its victim.

In fact, in order not to lose others' praises, we

prefer hidden and secret fasts to open ones, silence to eloquent speech, and being despised to being well-thought of. Alas, my God, it even manages, as we say, to stick its nose into such good practices as these, assaulting us with vain satisfactions.

St Jerome was right to compare vainglory to the shadow. The shadow follows the body around everywhere, and imitates its steps. Flee from it, and it flees too; walk slowly and it keeps pace; sit down and it does likewise (398).

350 Vainglory follows virtue everywhere [like the shadow of the body]. The body tries in vain to flee its shadow, it follows the body everywhere and keeps close. The same thing happens to anyone who has given themselves to virtue: the more they flee from vainglory the more they feel themselves besieged by it. Let all of us fear this great enemy of ours (398).

351 Let them keep hidden whatever good their Beloved is doing in them. The virtues are like a treasure: if it is not kept hidden from envious eyes it will be carried off. The devil is always vigilant. He is the worst of all the envious, and tries to steal this treasure of the virtues as soon as it is uncovered. He does this by assaulting us with this strong enemy, vainglory (399).

352 Our Lord, always concerned for our good, in order to keep us safe from this great enemy [vainglory], warns us about it in different parts of the Gospel. So he tells us that when we wish to pray, we should retire to our room, close the door and pray on our own, so that our prayer should not be known to others. And that when we fast we should

wash our faces, so that we don't let others know about it through our dirt and misery. And when we give alms, our right hand should not know what our left hand is doing (400).

353 They should take care never to speak about the things with which the good God is favouring them to anyone except their directors and confessors. Let them always direct all their actions for the glory of God, just as the Apostle desires: 'So, whether you eat or drink, or whatever you do, do everything for the glory of God.'[39]

They should renew this intention every now and again. They should examine themselves after the completion of every action, and when they recognise some imperfection, they shouldn't become troubled, but ashamed, and they should humble themselves before the goodness of God, asking the Lord for forgiveness and begging him to preserve them from this imperfection in the future (400).

354 Let them guard themselves from every vanity in their manner of dressing, because the Lord allows souls to fall for such vanity. Women who seek the vanity of clothing will never be able to clothe themselves in the life of Jesus Christ; the moment this idol enters their heart they lose every ornament of their souls. Their dress, as St Paul desired,[40] should be decent and modest, without braided hair, without gold, without gems, without costly clothes that might seem luxurious and present a display of magnificence (400).

---

39. 1 Cor 10:31.
40. Cf. 1 Tim 2:9.

355 I have this yet to add: keep watch over yourself and be always vigilant, especially regarding the cursed vice of vainglory – the worm, the woodworm of the devoted soul. There is a greater need to watch out for this vice because it finds it easier than the other vices to enter the soul unobserved, and is therefore very difficult to recognise. We should always be on the alert, and never think it too much to combat this tireless enemy, who is always on the lookout and watches our every action (576).

356 My God! What a torment the temptation to vainglory is. It seems of little importance, but we must convince ourselves that it actually is very important. Only by passing through this fire can we understand its great intensity (314).

357 Be calm concerning the progress of your soul. I only beg you to watch over the movements of your heart more wisely, and above all things to humble yourself before the majesty of the Lord, whose presence we should never try to leave. And let us watch that the devil does not worm his way into us, through the cursed vice of vainglory (680).

358 Thanks to the favours with which God continues to fill me, I have very much improved regarding my trust in God. It seemed to me at times in the past that I had need of others' help; this is no longer the case. I know through my own experience that the true remedy to prevent one from falling is to lean on the Cross of Christ, with confidence in him alone, who wished to be suspended from a cross for our salvation (463).

359 Let us constantly renew our faith and cry out with the humble patient of Idumea: "Lord, bring me close to you so that I might feel your presence, as you are close to me by your very nature, and if all hell were to be unleashed against me, I would not fear, nor would I be afraid"[41] (884).

360 Let us have faith that Jesus will always sustain us with his grace. Let us fight as strong souls with strong souls, and the reward will not be far off (598).

361 But enough of my crying out! It is good for whoever has the duty to keep quiet and is in the very depths of their defeat, to keep quiet! I despair of all, but not of him who is the life, the truth and the way. I ask him for everything and I abandon myself to him, because he was and is everything to me (1064).

362 O God, O God! I can say nothing else: 'Why have you abandoned me?' This spirit, justly smitten by your divine justice, finds itself in a violent contradiction, without anything to draw on or knowledge of what is happening, except fleeting insights, which serve only to sharpen the grief and torment. I feel that I'm dying, I burn with thirst, I grow faint with hunger, O Father. But it seems to me that this hunger has virtually reduced itself to a single desire: conformity to God's wishes, in exactly the way he desires (1037).

---

41. Translator's Note: There seems to be no such verse in the Book of Job in this form; cf. Job 14:13.

363 The wicked spirit is torturing me in every way. Will he be able to make a soul that has abandoned itself to God lose its way? I don't fear this at all. God's grace renders me powerful in all things (502).

364 There are moments in which the severity of Jesus comes to mind and I find myself becoming distressed. Then I set myself to consider his loving kindness and I am completely consoled. I cannot not abandon myself to this sweetness, this happiness...

What is it, Father, that I feel? I have such confidence in Jesus, that even if I were to see hell open up beneath my feet and find myself on the edge of the abyss, I would not lose faith, I would not despair; I would place my trust in him. Such is the confidence that his gentleness inspires in me (317).

365 Let them prostrate themselves before the Lord in humility of heart, as the King Jehoshaphat did when greatly oppressed and distressed by the great multitude of enemies that he saw himself encircled by, and let them raise their voices to him using the same words as that holy King: '*Cum ignoremus quid agere debeamus, hoc solum habemus residui ut oculos nostros dirigamus ad Te*',[42] not knowing, Lord, what to do, with no means available to us, not knowing how to avoid the danger, nothing remains for us to do except turn our eyes to you, so that you will come to help us in our need as best pleases you (434).

366 [Lack of confidence in the goodness of God] may be the finest of threads that binds the

---

42. 2 Chron 20:12, 'But as we know not what to do, we can only turn our eyes to you.'

spirit, it is true, but it greatly hampers the spirit in flying along the ways of perfection and in acting with holy freedom. We do great wrong to our heavenly Spouse by this lack of confidence; and in punishment for this, alas! the sweetest Lord deprives us of many graces because the doors of our hearts are not opened to him with holy confidence. If the soul doesn't decide to have done with this attitude, it will bring down many punishments on its head. Let this assertion of mine not seem exaggerated, dear Father (406).

367 Scorn the deceits of those impure apostates, with boundless confidence take refuge in the shade of the divine Spouse, and fear nothing. The burning rays of Lucifer cannot penetrate the shade provided by such a dense leaf-canopy, and even if they do, you need not fear that you will be burnt by them. The very rays that seek to harm us, in fact, help us to walk with ever increasing fear and love. And so where Satan tried to make us lose our way, he helps us gain new treasures of paradise (379).

368 I am not frightened; do I not have a Father in Jesus? Is it not true that I will always be his son? I can say with certainty that Jesus has never forgotten me, even when I was far from him. His love has followed me everywhere (334).

369 Spiritual troubles and warfare, I assure you, go hand in hand with bodily afflictions. As one set multiplies, so the other augments. I don't know where I will end up, if things continue this way. I thank the Lord, however, because although I suffer moments of great agony (and particularly so in certain encounters), I always maintain – even though I must

do great violence to myself – a joyful spirit, and it seems to me that a new courage descends sweetly into my heart.

So I cast myself with trust into the arms of Jesus, and when all the things he himself decreed actually happen, he can hardly refuse to help me (214).

370 My Father, it is true that I feel very weak, but I'm not afraid, since Jesus must surely see my anxieties and the burden that oppresses me? Did he not tell us through the mouth of the royal prophet: 'He knows our weaknesses... He is like a Father, full of tenderness for his children... The Lord is merciful to us'.[43] Well, the Lord consoles me in my weakness, and makes me rejoice 'in my weakness'[44].

371 My Father, when will the sun shine in the heaven of my soul? Alas! I am lost in the deep dark night through which I pass. But long live God! He never abandons anyone who hopes and trusts in him! (800).

372 Storm follows storm, and the peace I am waiting for is long in coming. But since everything is ordered with wisdom, I strive with the highest point of the spirit to resign myself, to offer my *fiat*, though I do this without in any way feeling spiritually refreshed (787).

373 What must I tell you about myself? My soul sustains a continual struggle. I see no other escape than to abandon myself into the arms of Jesus.

---

43. Cf. Ps 103:13-14.
44. Cf. 2 Cor 12:9.

Jesus often allows me to sleep in these arms. Blessed sleep! Sleep that joyfully restores the soul after the struggles it has sustained (485).

374 I feel a strong impulse to abandon myself entirely to providence and not to worry about anything, whether favourable or unfavourable, and all this happened without any care or anxiety.

Before I used to feel ashamed at the thought that others might come to know about what the Lord has been doing in me, but for some time now it hasn't bothered me. This is because I see that I am no better for these favours – I am worse even – and draw little profit from these graces (423).

375 Oh, how well protected is the soul that God has gathered under his wings. Yes, it can take its seat and rest in total peace in this shade, because he who fills it with so many graces will not allow it to fall. Jesus wants it entirely for himself. Let this precious gem revive its faith and cast itself with sublime abandon into the arms of God, and God will fulfil his plans for it (379).

376 Oh God! grant me a little hope so that in the end I might come to reflect you, and see you as you are, my God, my All, the God of my soul, purified and remade in the crucible of your just severity! (1097).

377 When the storm rages at its height and an overflowing measure of my wretchedness crushes me, I am powerless to raise myself up on the happy wings of hope, a virtue so necessary for abandonment in God (1036).

378 The trials of my spirit grow ever more intense. But long live God! who even in the midst of trials does not allow the soul to lose its way. I suffer, but I am certain that in the midst of the suffering and pitch darkness in which my spirit is continually plunged, hope will not fail (918).

379 Ah! my Father, I don't want to despair, because I don't wish to wrong divine compassion. But I feel death penetrating into the innermost parts of my being! Help me, Father, and God will not allow me to succumb (1255).

380 My God! I don't want, no, to despair; I don't want to wrong your infinite compassion. But despite all my efforts to trust, I have inside me a terrible, vivid and clear sense of your abandonment and rejection.

My God! I trust in you; but this trust is full of agitation, and this renders my grief even more bitter.

O my God! If I could know even in the least way that my present state is not due to your rejection and that I am not offending you, I would be willing to suffer a hundred times this torment. My God, my God… have mercy on me (1264).

381 I strive to hope and I become tempted by presumption. My God, what can I do? I hope, and I am tempted by presumption. I am frightened, terrified and reduced to helplessness by the thought that I can hope no more (1222).

382 The uncertainty of my future oppresses me, but I nurture a lively hope that I will see my dreams realised, because the Lord would not place any thoughts and longings in a soul that he didn't wish to really come true, nor would he fail to satisfy any longings a soul has, which he himself was the author of (662).

383 God wishes to marry the soul in faith, and the soul that celebrates this heavenly marriage must walk in pure faith, which is the only means suitable for this union of love (441).

384 Pardon my folly, O Father: I am about to be submerged and drowned in the full height of the filthy waters. I can hardly take any more. I feel everything failing, except for that tenuous thread which is faith, and which is the only thing I have to hold onto in this tempestuous sea (634).

385 I have come to the realisation that I barely have the strength to sustain the struggle. I am dying of hunger in front of a richly-spread table; I am burning with thirst below the spring which flows with pure water... What more? the light blinds me before clearing away the fog that surrounds me. How come? I am tired of tiring my guide and all that supports me, and obedience alone prevents me from giving in completely. Because of this [obedience] I undertake to reveal what is happening in me (1065).

386 I am lost, yes, lost in the unknown. I am bereft of everything. But I am resolved, even though I experience no comfort, to stay close to the one who acts in the place of God (1030).

387 I fear my heart, it does not know what is truly wicked. One who has a firm purpose resists obeying blindly (1088).

388 Father, forgive me these digressions. I am unable to reason any more, I can no longer subdue my reason and my heart. My life has ebbed away, and the death which strangles my soul prevents anything from clinging on to life, and nothing is able to dissipate this deadly sleep. I stick to – or rather I seem to stick to, and I don't know how – the help that you have thus far given me (1028).

389 The Spiritual desolations are insufferable; they pursue me ever more closely. Authority alone sustains me in the midst of so much darkness (830).

390 I wish to – and I strive continually in this desire even just for the sake of rendering my almost desperate position a little less desperate – follow the instructions that my guide has given me. But what happens? Even saying the *Creed* constitutes an atrocious martyrdom, but when I must actually profess it, there is a bitterness which remains in the depths of my soul, and my soul having extinguished the created light now sees no other type of light at all (1097).

391 Obedience is everything to me, but I experience no comfort in placing myself under obedience. May God help me, if I were, with my eyes open, to transgress in any matter that had been allotted to me by any judge, whether external or internal. And yet why am I so full of fears on this

point? Tell me, for charity's sake, how am I to behave in this situation? (807).

392 I strive to keep hold of the assurances made by whoever acts in the place of God, but no ray of light ever descends into my soul. A dry belief, without any comfort and which is only sufficient to keep the soul from being cast into despair (751).

393 My one regret is that, without wanting to or noticing that I am doing it, it happens sometimes that I raise my voice a little in matters touching on correction. I know this is a reprehensible weakness, but how can I avoid it, if it happens without my noticing it? And yet I pray, groan and complain to our Lord about it; he has not yet answered me fully. Even though I keep a vigilant lookout for this fault, I sometimes do what I loathe and want to avoid doing (1170).

394 That fine lady, sweet-temperedness, seems to be doing a bit better; but I'm not satisfied. I don't want to lose heart, however. I have made many promises to Jesus and Mary, my Father! Through their help I desire to practise this virtue; and in exchange, other than keeping up the other promises I have made them, I have promised to meditate faithfully on this same virtue and to talk to souls about it.

You see, Father, that I am not indifferent to the practice of this virtue. Help me with your prayers and the prayers of others (1244).

395 Let us humble ourselves greatly, my good Father, and let us confess that if God were not our breastplate and shield, we would immediately

be pierced through by every sort of sin. For this we must always keep ourselves in God with perseverance in our Spiritual exercises and learn to serve God at our own expense (916).

396 I beg you to be constant in the inner exercise that you write to me about. Believe me, Father, your present state is nothing other than one of a true 'insensitivity', which deprives you of the enjoyment of not only consolations and inspiration but even of faith, hope and charity. Although you have been entrusted with these things, you derive no consolation from them, you are like a child who has a guardian. The guardian takes care of the administration of the child's goods so that the child, although it is the owner of the property, actually has no control over it and seems to possess nothing but its own life, as St. Paul says: 'Though he is the owner of all the estate, he is no better than a slave'.[45] For God does not wish you to feel the love of God or of neighbour in any perceptible way, nor to enjoy these loves beyond what is necessary in each occasion.

You should consider yourself fortunate in being held so closely by your heavenly guardian. You have to do nothing else than persevere in your Spiritual exercises and abandon yourself into the arms of this most compassionate guardian (916).

397 Jesus is pleased to communicate himself to simple souls. Let us strive to acquire this beautiful virtue, let us hold it in great esteem. Jesus said: 'unless you become like children, you will never

---

45. Gal 4:1.

enter the kingdom of heaven.'[46] But before teaching this to us through words he practised it himself in deed. He became a child, and gave us an example of that simplicity which he then taught with words.

Let us serve our hearts with an eviction order, holding them far from any earthly prudence. Let us strive to have a mind that is always pure in its thoughts, just in its thoughts, holy in its intentions. Let us guard our wills and not allow them to seek anything other than God and his glory.

If we strive to progress in this beautiful virtue, he who taught us it will continually enrich us with new insights and greater heavenly favours (607).

---

46. Mt 18:3.

XII

SCATTERED FLOWERS

It is not easy to reduce all the richness, the variety of teaching, the experiences and all the advice scattered throughout the life-giving pages of Padre Pio's correspondence into distinct and well-defined categories.

In the desire to enrich this anthology as much as possible, this chapter will present a collection of maxims and writings that could not be gathered together under a common heading because of their independence and variety.

The following brief thoughts, as will be clear to anyone who reads them, were inspired by feasts or liturgical seasons, community or religious events, current or social affairs. Padre Pio's interest in the events connected to the war that involved many of his religious brothers in Italy, not excluding his own Spiritual directors, is a notable example of such an inspiration.

We present this rather jumbled-up collection of thoughts in no particular order, because each one can be the object of in-depth personal reflection in itself.

398 May Jesus be the star that always guides our feet through the desert of this present life and lead us without delay to the door of salvation (1180).

399 You propose, my good Father, always to respond generously to the Lord, making yourself worthy of him – that is, like him – in the adorable perfections recorded in the Scriptures and the Gospels. But in order for this imitation to happen, it is necessary to reflect daily on the life of him who proposes himself as a model to us. From reflection is born esteem for his acts, and from esteem the desire for and comfort of the imitation (1000).

400 May I never lose, O dear Jesus, the most precious treasure of yourself. My Lord and my God, that ineffable sweetness that pours from your eyes has become too vividly impressed on my soul, my Good; you deigned to look on this poor wretch with eyes of love.

How, then, can the agony of my heart be lessened, knowing myself far from you? My soul knows only too well what a terrible battle I waged when you, O my Beloved, hid yourself from me. What a terrible and thunderous impression all this left on my soul! (675).

401 O how good is Jesus, my dearest Father! It is true that he is good to all, but he is particularly good to those who strive to love him with all their heart (967).

402 It is true, of course, that Jesus hides himself very often. But what does it matter? I will try with his help to stay always close to him, you yourself having assured me that these absences are not abandonment but the pranks that lovers play (198).

403 I am the plaything of the Child Jesus, as he himself often says to me. But what is worse is that Jesus has chosen a toy of no value. I am sorry only that the toy he chose dirties his divine hands. It sometimes occurs to me that one day I will throw myself into a ditch to stop me trifling with you. I would relish it; I deserve nothing other than this (331).

404 If we strive to love Jesus, this alone will cast out every fear from us, and the soul will feel that it does not walk in the ways of the Lord, but flies. The soul is in such a state that it is led to cry out with the royal Prophet: 'I run the way of your commandments, for you enlarge my understanding.'[47]

405 How difficult, my Father, is the way of Christian perfection for a badly-disposed soul like mine! My wickedness makes me afraid at every step I take. May the good God prevent me from becoming unfaithful to him! (557).

406 To make God look more favourably on my poor prayers, I will strive, with divine grace, to be a good religious priest so that one day I will be able to say with the Apostle without any fear of lying: 'Be imitators of me, as I am of Christ.'[48] This I have promised to do with Jesus' help. I do not, alas, merit such help from him, but his inexhaustible charity towards us gives me hope (556).

---

47. Ps 119:32.
48. 1 Cor 11:1; cf. also 4:16.

407 Those *Cossacks* are trying to torment me in every possible way. When I complain to Jesus about this, I sense him repeating to me: 'Courage, because peace follows the battle'.

He tells me that I need faith and love. I am ready for anything, and ready to do his will. Only pray, I beg you, that I might spend this little bit of life that is left to me for his glory and that his light may be spread through me (328).

408 I tell the Lord about the things I am continually discovering in my life: work; reform of life; my Spiritual resurrection; true, substantial love; the sincere conversion of my entire self to him (558).

409 If I am sober with others, it's because I fear that too much talking might cause me to do wrong (590).

410 Perhaps I am deluding myself miserably when I see God so clearly in the centre of my heart! O my Father, who will assure me completely that I am not separated from that most tender Spouse of souls? Ouch! How hard life is! how painful it is, how bitter! keeping us in permanent uncertainty regarding what is most important for us to know in this exile here below! I cannot see who could possibly desire it, while the only comfort that one could expect from it – that of giving pleasure to God in everything – is so uncertain and open to so many dangers! (662).

411 Other types of revelations and apparitions concern Our Lord in human form: at the Last Supper, perspiring blood in the garden, bound to the column, glorious and resplendent in his Resurrection, and yet other forms. Yet other types concern the Queen of Angels and other heavenly persons clothed in human form.

The soul is able in a certain fashion to talk about such things, but prefers to withdraw into a perfect silence. It withdraws because it finds the great gap between what it saw (and has still present) and what it is actually able to describe, very painful. It seems to this soul that such noble subjects are very badly treated (375).

412 Therefore do not fear. You are suffering, of course, and will continue to suffer. But shouldn't it comfort a soul to know that such sufferings are a sign of divine love? to know that all these griefs are acceptable to God's heart? (643).

413 A soul that is overflowing with grief never finds it too much to express its grief at great length; in so doing it reveals its wounds to the one who has been charged by God to guide it (651).

414 How fortunate are those souls that are written in the book of eternal life! A thousand times fortunate are those souls who are the favourites of God's Heart! (650).

415 How beautiful are the souls in which the heavenly spouse reigns! If such a beauty were to be shown to all, one would not see our many foolish brothers run to where God is not to be found (389).

416 We must continually beg our sweetest Lord that two things grow in us: love and fear,

because one will make us fly in the ways of the Lord, and the other will make us watch where we put our feet; the first will allow us to see the things of this world for what they are, the second will make us guard ourselves from any negligence. When love and fear embrace, it is no longer in our power to place our affections on the things here below. There would be no more quarrels or envy. Our only dream on this earth would be to make the object of our love happy. We would feel ourselves dying from the desire to be loved by him. We would feel ready to sacrifice our lives, if by such a sacrifice we might render ourselves more pleasing in his eyes (407).

417 I know my wretchedness, and I am filled with shame. I know what favours God has granted me and I feel my soul bursting apart, because I know also that I am becoming ever more unworthy.

Oh! if only this most tender Spouse would deign either to cease his favours, or to raise up my fragile nature; otherwise I will die of it all, I cannot take any more! (418).

418 But, my Father, even though I do not know who this good for whom my heart avidly searches actually is, it seems to me that I do know very clearly the following: this good is inexhaustible, it is boundless. It seems to me, furthermore, that I understand my heart could never contain it, because in my ignorance I feel that it is a very great good, an immense good, an infinite good. Could this be Jesus? (358)

419 May the flames of divine love grow ever more greatly in your heart, and consume all

that doesn't know Jesus! May the divine Master make the sweetness of his most loving invitation ever more penetrate your being, the invitation that he addresses to all the souls wishing to follow him: 'My yoke is easy, and my burden light'[49] (529).

420 Anyway, let that be as it is, I am ready to suffer everything for the triumph of God's glory. It would be enough for me not to be separated by him from his love (531).

421 May our heavenly Father, who has dealt with me thus, be ever blessed. May he be glorified also in my body, since he is my life, and I live only to serve him. I do not live for myself, I live only for him (497).

422 Let us pray together to the most sweet Comforter of true lovers like this: 'O God, most sweet repose of those who love you, Oh! allow a heart that lives only to be wanted by you to finally taste this repose. You alone can render less severe the martyrdom of a soul that is torn apart by the desire to unite itself to you forever (641).

423 I find that if a conversation is prolonged for the sake of recreation, and if I am unable to withdraw from it, I really have to force myself not to leave, and both the conversation and the effort cause me great grief (43).

424 I will try to describe to you the effect Jesus has on me using the following rough

---

49. Mt 11:30.

comparison. In the way that a strong current in the depths of the sea drags everything it encounters on its path after itself, so my soul, immersed in the shoreless ocean of Jesus' love draws – without any merit on my part or my being able to account for it – all his treasures behind itself (297).

425 May the heavenly Child help you to experience in your heart all the holy emotions that he granted me to feel in that blessed night, when he was laid down in that poor shed!

O God! my Father, I wouldn't know how to express to you all I felt in my heart on that most happy night. I felt my heart overflowing with a holy love towards our God become man. Even then night still enveloped my spirit; but it must be recorded that in the midst of such a pitch darkness I suffered from an extremely bad case of Spiritual indigestion. O how many times did my thoughts go from the Child to yourself, and from yourself to the Child!

I wouldn't know how to recount to you all that happened in me on this night, which I spent in its entirety on my feet and without ever closing an eye! (981).

426 As the holy time of Easter draws near, I feel more than ever the duty to wish you a most joyful Easter in the sweet Jesus. I pray continually for you and you are always foremost in my prayers. But during these most holy days, when it seems that divine compassion is more disposed to hear the prayers of the soul that hopes in it, confides in it and abandons itself to it, I will pray with confidence for the fulfilment of all the vows you made with your heart – and not least of all, the vow of perfect and complete abandonment into the arms of its divine goodness (1270).

427 May Jesus reign always as sovereign in your heart, may he help you fulfil all the vows you have made, may he fill you with ever greater graces; and not least of all, may he grant you the grace of making all become tranquil within you and around you, and bring you to rest without fear on his Fatherly heart! This, in a few brief words, is the essence of the offerings that I make continually to Jesus for you, but with a greater intensity and fervour I promise again to offer them to Jesus on your patron saint's day, through the saint whose name you bear.

May you be pleased to accept my sincere wishes and offerings, my Father, as the true expression of all the affection and gratitude that I have for you in Jesus (1267).

428 May Jesus always be the sovereign king of your heart, may he assist you always with his watchful grace, may he make his divine love grow continually in your soul, may he transform you completely into himself, and may he make you holy.

Here, in brief, are the offerings that I make continually to the Lord for you, but which I will repeat with a greater eagerness and confidence on your patron saint's day and on the holy feast of Easter.

May it please Jesus to hear all the offerings that I am making for you! And may it please you, Father, to accept them, because they come from a heart that loves you sincerely in Jesus (1215).

429 May Jesus be always yours entirely, may you possess him in heaven forever, as you now possess him sacramentally every day in your hands and in your heart, and may he make you ever more worthy of his divine embraces.

This is, in brief, the essence of the offerings that I make continually for you, but which I will make with even greater eagerness on your patron saint's day.

May it please him to answer all of them. For your part, Father, accept them as the sincere expression of the affection and gratitude that I bear you (1240).

430 May Jesus always watch over you with a benevolent eye, may he be always and in everything your escort, sustainer and guide, and make you worthy always of his love! These are the offerings that I make continually to Jesus for you. I will continue to make these, and other, offerings for you before the Child Jesus. Accept these offerings and wishes of mine, Father, that come from the heart of one who loves you sincerely in Jesus (1188).

431 May the heavenly Child smile on your spirit, which groans beneath the blows of divine compassion! And may that light which flooded the minds of the devout shepherds of Bethlehem illuminate your mind also, and never abandon you, if that is what is best for your spirit! (1195).

432 May the Child Jesus descend into your heart this night and fill it entirely with his divine love (1254).

433 May the newborn Child fill your heart with superabundant grace and render it ever more worthy of himself! May the peaceful king speed the day of victory and peace. We are drawing near to the feast of the holy Child and I send you my best wishes.

My wish for you is that the Child of Bethlehem may strengthen your heart in the fire of divine love and adorn your soul with the most noble virtues (973).

434 On the feast of the divine Infant, I'm not promising that I will increase my prayers for you, because this I do continually, but I will strive to pray with greater fervour. I will pray to the divine Child in a special way so that he might make you grow ever more in charity and will instil into your spirit the light of heavenly wisdom. I will pray that you might grow in the spirit of heavenly wisdom regarding three mysteries in particular: the mystery of our Christian vocation, that of the eternal treasures that he has reserved for us, and the mystery of our justification (516).

435 My Father, when will this cruel slaughter come to an end? It seems that my soul has been stripped of every trace of the beauty that comes from grace; and deprived of this adornment which is so vital to it, left with nothing but its own abilities, it has almost sunk to the level of the brute beasts (1039).

436 My God, lead me to repentance, treat me with your harsh medicine that leads to sincere contrition and firm conversion of heart to you (1075).

437 Every time we become perturbed is very displeasing indeed to Jesus. This is because such disturbances are never unaccompanied by imperfection and always have their origin in selfishness and self-love (608).

438 During this hour, so solemn for our own Italy, for Europe and for the entire world, Jesus does not allow me to experience a moment of Spiritual refreshment. We are living through a time of not only national, but also world-wide sorrow; it would not be right, then, for any soul to derive even a moment's joy from the fact that it is not on the field of battle beside its brother (594).

439 Let us pray, my Father, for the cessation of hostilities. Let us disarm the arm of the divine judge, justly angered with the nations, who want nothing to do with the law of love (495).

440 The horrors of the war have almost unsettled my mind. My soul has been placed in an extreme desolation. Though I had been preparing myself for it, I was unable to prevent the terror and desolation gripping tight hold of my soul.

This blessed war really will have a wholesome and purifying influence on our Italy and the Church of God. Faith will reawaken in the Italian heart. Faith is already there, but it is hidden, and drowsy and suffocated by wills inclined to wickedness. This war will make the most beautiful flowers blossom in the Church of God, in a land almost entirely arid and dry. But my God! before this happens, a severe trial is reserved for us. We must pass through an entire night shrouded in the thickest darkness, the like of which has never been seen before our own time (583).

441 Jesus wishes thus to prolong our communal martyrdom [the war], and may he always be blessed. The hour through which we are passing is a solemn one. Up to now we have remained strangers to the sorrowful war that has been fought for nearly a year; those who in these difficult times represent the constituted authority and who guide the destiny of our homeland, call all of us to fulfil the painful duty which presents itself in the form of this war.

We must all do our duty, according to our strengths. We must accept, with a serene spirit and with courage, the orders that come to us from above. If our homeland calls us, we must obey its command; if this call imposes painful trials on us, let us accept them with resignation and courage. We may shed tears of a suffering that tears us apart, but let them be resigned tears.

The trial is hard for all, but more than ever it is hard for us. But let us lift our hearts on high, to God; from him we will receive strength, peace, comfort. We must all co-operate for the common good in this difficult hour, and appease God's mercy, with humble and fervent prayer and with the amendment of our lives (587).

442 Courage, Father, because the rainbow of peace will not be long in shining on the blood-stained soul of all of Europe! The Lord is still angered by humanity's iniquities, but he will certainly not judge us with the full rigour of his justice (813).

XIII

'ONE THING ALONE REMAINS, MY FRIEND: DEATH'

(*Letters*, volume 1, p. 767)

Death is a frequently recurring theme in Padre Pio's letters. He talks of death in different ways, with different emphases, and for various reasons.

We mustn't think, however, that his ardent desire to leave this valley of tears was motivated by either the terrible physical sufferings caused by his poor health, or the somewhat selfish – though very human and natural – desire to free himself from the many sufferings and anxiety of a moral nature he experienced. Even less was this desire the result of a pessimistic or Manichean view of human life on earth.

Padre Pio's desire can be explained by the joint action of two forces which come originally from different sources but end up working in unison: a 'centrifugal' force that impels us to avoid moral evil, and a 'centripetal' force that draws us to unite ourselves with what is good. This can be explained as follows: Padre Pio did not know whether he would be able to persevere in love or avoid displeasing God by growing cold towards him and becoming unfaithful – this led him to desire the end of his exile, where he would no longer have the opportunity to sin; but equally he experienced an insatiable longing and fervent yearning to be united to the Beloved and lose himself in the ocean of God, this desire consumed his physical energies, and lifted him up to God with its vigorous and irresistible wind beats – so for another very different reason he longed to return to his Father's house.

In these passages we find the genuine and passionate language of the mystic and the sincere and profound aspirations of the saint.

❧❦❧

443 O life, how cruel you are to me! How long you are! O life, you are no longer life for me, but a torment! O death, I don't know who could fear you; through you, life is opened to us! (384).

444 O life, you are too long! O life, you are cruel! O life, you are no longer life for me! Oh, how I feel alone, my God and my sweetest Saviour, in this desert of the world! Do you not see that my malady is without cure? I think I am forever destined to pine away for you... (656).

445 How happy I would be to be consumed as quickly as possible by this flame! O yes, the compassionate Jesus will reveal himself finally to those who search ardently for him: and since no one can see him without dying, let him kill me too – I would consider myself most happy, because the gain is far greater than the loss (471).

446 My soul eagerly longs to see itself totally possessed by this great God, whose love it feels has stolen and has transfixed its heart. The poor thing bears further delays of the fulfilment of its ardent desire unwillingly. It can no longer resist the pain that torments it (471).

447 My life has become a great burden to me, because it deprives me of true life. I know, because the Lord prolongs my life, that this is his will. And yet I am never able, despite all my strivings, to make an act of true resignation – having continually before my mind's eye the knowledge that it is only through death that one finds true life (655).

448 Poor soul! Already it is tired of watching its Spouse – who has robbed it of everything – through the *crystal fountain*. It has so far seen the features of its Spouse in, as it were, outline form only and now it wants to see them in their fullness and perfection. In a word, it wants it to see the Word, the Son of God, who is the splendour of God's glory and the perfect image of his substance.

Ask resolutely, I beg you, that Jesus put an end to so much torment. Ask him to uncover and reveal his beauty, his divine essence, to the poor butterfly; and so may he finally kill it – and in doing so he will liberate it from the chains of the flesh, because in the flesh it can neither see its God, nor rejoice in him as it desires (471).

449 Place before the eyes of this most tender Spouse the continual martyrdom that his great love makes this poor soul suffer. Tell him with great faith that this torment can only cease through the glorious vision of his divine essence. Tell him that there is no longer a remedy for my pain, beyond that of his presence and sight. Let him no longer, then, distract this poor soul with other communications because these cannot satisfy its desire and its will. May he finally give himself totally through a union of perfect and consummated love (472).

450 Living here below, my Father, wearies me. Living this life of exile is such a bitter torment to me that I am almost unable to take any more. The thought that in any instant I could lose Jesus, causes me an anxiety that I cannot explain; only the soul that loves Jesus sincerely could understand it (328).

451 I desire death only because it will unite me with indissoluble chains to the heavenly Spouse (357).

452 While I was reciting the Lord's prayer, before I had pronounced the words 'Libera nos a malo', I felt myself seized by so strong an impulse that, despite all my efforts to suppress it, my soul felt itself transported as if to another place; and there it asked the Heavenly One with the greatest ardour to be liberated from all evil – the present life. My soul understood in an instant that it would find no relief from its evils in this life, this life being so far from such a great good – its Beloved. For this reason, it asked our heavenly Father with a most intense ardour to free it from this greatest evil – life – and to bring it into the heavenly homeland near its God.

This impulse came upon me in an instant, and I believe that I could not have survived if the experience were to have continued a little longer (419).

453 Alas! my Father, how difficult is this mortal life! As long as this life lasts, eternal life is uncertain! O cruel life, enemy of my Love –who loves us infinitely more than we could love him or know him. Oh! why is it not given to us to bring you to an end? O life, for the creature which has come to know

its Lover, you are no longer life! This creature here endures you in peace, because God endures you, it takes care of you, because you are his gift. But you should at least not be treacherous or ungrateful to the poor thing! (682).

454 My Father, who is more wretched than this creature? It has already tightly bound its capacity for free choice, that unhappy slave of its freedom, to the chain of fear and love of the God who created it. But this is not enough, it wants to feel itself bound to him by another love, a love that cannot be realised in this world here below. It wants to enter without delay into its eternal rest, so that it can live forever lost in that immense ocean of goodness and know only what he loves and rejoice where he himself is blessed (682).

455 You wrote in your letter: 'It seems to me that the end of your earthly exile might not be far off'; this thought made me come out of myself. It brought my reading of your letter to a halt; I felt my sufferings, which are unbearable, lighten for an instant; I felt my lungs enlarging and taking in a pure and cooling air; I felt this life-giving air penetrate all the fibres, run through my veins and enliven every globule, every molecule of blood.

I felt a very sweet rapture, a quietening of the spirit and the body, pure like the clearest sky, and it made me exclaim from the bottom of my soul: 'O what a wonderful dawn this is! O how wonderful it is to close the eyes of the body and open those of the spirit before the divine Spouse! One feels so well!

I sense death very clearly, full of elasticity; the heart free and wide like the sea. The thoughts that troubled me, the biting cares, the weariness of life, all that bitterness, annoyances, dryness, disillusionments, griefs that fill my soul with anxiety – all disappeared as if by a magic spell, I didn't even remember them (716).

456 At other times, without my even thinking of it, a most vivid desire to possess Jesus entirely enkindles itself in my soul. Then, with a clarity such as the Lord gives when he communicates with my soul and that I wouldn't know how to put in writing, he makes me see my entire future earthly life as if in a mirror – it is nothing but a torment. I yearn for death with an ineffable ardour, without being able to explain it to myself. I am impelled despite all my efforts to ask God with tears to be taken from this exile (367).

457 Another year disappears into eternity, burdened by all the wrongs I committed during that time. How many souls more fortunate than I have entered the house of Jesus, and there they will rest forever! How many most happy souls, which I envy, have passed into eternity, dying the death of the just, kissed by Jesus, comforted by the sacraments, assisted by a minister of God, with a heavenly smile on their lips – in spite of all the torments of physical suffering by which they were oppressed! (328).

458 Calvary is the mount of the saints; but from there you pass to another mount, which is called Tabor. But when will this day come? When will we sing the hymn of victory over all our enemies? When will we be allowed to intone the Alleluia? Alas! it will be a long time yet; justice has not

yet been done. Long live God, and may his justice be done! (830).

459 Alas! What has happened to me? Wherever I turn, I find thorns which bite into me. One thing alone: death. I call on it by day and I call on it by night with the single aim of receiving some relief from all my misfortunes. Am I wrong to desire this? Tell me frankly. I should warn you, however, my Father, that when I do not seek death I am not really liberated from myself. It is a cry that rises spontaneously from my lips without my being able to keep it back, and this I see harms me. Perhaps there is a secret hope lying hidden in the depths of my soul, whose luminous ray will appear suddenly from the dust (767).

460 I must tell you that I sacrifice myself willingly for the hope I have that one day in this mortal life I will sing with the royal Prophet: 'Lord, you have finally loosened my bonds, and because of this I will offer you a sacrifice of praise for all eternity'[50] (906).

---

50. Cf. Ps 116:16-17.

CORONCINA
TO THE SACRED HEART OF JESUS

I   O my Jesus, you said, 'In truth I tell you, ask and you will receive, seek, and you will find, knock and it will be opened to you', and so I knock, I seek, I ask for the grace of...
Our Father, Hail Mary, Glory be.
Sacred Heart of Jesus, I hope and trust in you.

II   O my Jesus, you said, 'In truth I tell you, whatever you ask my Father for in my name, he will give you', and so in your name I ask your Father for the grace of...
Our Father, Hail Mary, Glory be.
Sacred Heart of Jesus, I hope and trust in you.

III   O my Jesus, you said, 'In truth I tell you, the heavens and the earth will pass away, but my words will never pass away', and so trusting in the unfailing truth of your holy words I ask for the grace of...
Our Father, Hail Mary, Glory be.
Sacred Heart of Jesus, I hope and trust in you.

O Sacred Heart of Jesus, for whom it is impossible not to have compassion on those who are wretched, have mercy on us poor sinners, and grant us the graces that we request through the Immaculate Heart of Mary, your tender mother and ours.

St Joseph, putative father of the Sacred Heart of Jesus, pray for us. *Salve Regina.*

NB: This coroncina was recited every day by Padre Pio for all those who commended themselves to his prayers. For this reason the faithful are invited to recite it daily in order to unite themselves spiritually to the prayer of the blessed Father.

About Paraclete Press

WHO WE ARE

Paraclete Press is a publisher of books, recordings, and DVDs on Christian spirituality. Our publishing represents a full expression of Christian belief and practice—from Catholic to Evangelical, from Protestant to Orthodox.

We are the publishing arm of the Community of Jesus, an ecumenical monastic community in the Benedictine tradition. As such, we are uniquely positioned in the marketplace without connection to a large corporation and with informal relationships to many branches and denominations of faith.

WHAT WE ARE DOING

BOOKS | Paraclete publishes books that show the richness and depth of what it means to be Christian. Although Benedictine spirituality is at the heart of all that we do, we publish books that reflect the Christian experience across many cultures, time periods, and houses of worship. We publish books that nourish the vibrant life of the church and its people—books about spiritual practice, formation, history, ideas, and customs.

We have several different series, including the best-selling Living Library, Paraclete Essentials, and Paraclete Giants series of classic texts in contemporary English; A Voice from the Monastery—men and women monastics writing about living a spiritual life today; award-winning literary faith fiction and poetry; and the Active Prayer Series that brings creativity and liveliness to any life of prayer.

RECORDINGS | From Gregorian chant to contemporary American choral works, our music recordings celebrate sacred choral music through the centuries. Paraclete distributes the recordings of the internationally acclaimed choir Gloriæ Dei Cantores, praised for their "rapt and fathomless spiritual intensity" by American Record Guide, and the Gloriæ Dei Cantores Schola, which specializes in the study and performance of Gregorian chant. Paraclete is also the exclusive North American distributor of the recordings of the Monastic Choir of St. Peter's Abbey in Solesmes, France, long considered to be a leading authority on Gregorian chant.

DVDS | Our DVDs offer spiritual help, healing, and biblical guidance for life issues: grief and loss, marriage, forgiveness, anger management, facing death, and spiritual formation.

LEARN MORE ABOUT US AT OUR WEB SITE:
www.paracletepress.com, or call us toll-free at 1-800-451-5006.

You may also be interested in...

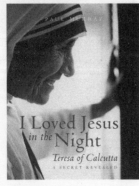

*"To be in love & yet not to love,
to live by faith and yet not to believe.
To spend myself
and yet to be in total darkness."*
—TERESA OF CALCUTTA

Paul Murray
ISBN: 978-1-55725-579-2
$18.95 in hardcover

I Loved Jesus in the Night is one priest's compelling account of meeting the saint of Calcutta. Sharing anecdotes and first-hand experiences, Paul Murray offers a glimpse into why Mother Teresa could declare in one of her letters, that if ever she were to "become a saint," she would surely be one of "darkness." These intimate reflections on her "private writings" illumine the meaning of a life that is only now beginning to be understood.

PAUL MURRAY O.P. is an Irish Dominican, poet, and professor in Rome at the University of St Thomas, the "Angelicum."

*Spend Christmas
in the good company
of the Holy Fathers*

Compiled by Peter Celano
Foreword by Thomas Howard
ISBN: 978-1-55725-603-4
$17.95 in hardcover

"I am an old Christmas person and cannot imagine a more spiritual and impressive way than spending the Christmas season with the popes. This is a marvelous book to give anyone who has a real sense of the Church and of the significance of the teachings of the bishops of Rome. I highly recommend it."
—FR. BENEDICT J. GROESCHEL, C.F.R., author & TV host on EWTN

Available from most booksellers or through Paraclete Press:
www.paracletepress.com; 1-800-451-5006. Try your local bookstore first.